Illustrated History of
GOLF

Illustrated History of
GOLF

Mitchell Platts

Portland House
A Division of Crown Publishers, Inc.
A Bison Book

This 1988 edition published by
Portland House, distributed by
Crown Publishers, Inc.
225 Park Avenue South
New York, NY 10003

Produced by
Bisons Books Corp.
15 Sherwood Place
Greenwich, CT 06830
USA

Printed in Italy

Library of Congress Cataloging-in-Publication Data
Platts, Mitchell.
  The illustrated history of golf/by Mitchell Platts.
    p.   cm.
  ISBN 0-517-65837-2
  1. Golf—History.   2. Golfers—Biography.   I. Title.
GV963.P53   1988   87-34785
796.352'09—dc19   CIP

For my mother and father

PAGE 1: *St Andrews.*
PAGES 2-3: *Royal Troon.*
PAGES 4-5: *Hoylake, Royal Liverpool, 1933.*

Contents

Introduction

The game of golf possesses a magical, almost mystical, power to entice men and women into making an unnatural movement of the body. This movement of swinging a club can cause not only physical suffering but mental anguish. Since the sole purpose of this act is to hit a little white ball around a field, booby-trapped with bunkers, hedgerows, water hazards and towering trees, with the intention of delivering it to a hole $4\frac{1}{4}$ inches in diameter, there must be many people who view golfers as foolhardy. The game can reduce a perfectly sane human being, simply wishing to escape momentarily from the hysteria of daily life behind an office desk, into a veritable nervous wreck.

But once captivated by the game of golf, no player can resist the challenge. Many a lunch has been spoiled and many a partner has been widowed by the game, because of a 19th hole examination. The happy hacker wants the world to hear about the three iron which, in the course of the other 108 shots he struck, flew unerringly to the hole with all the authority of a professional hit.

Yet there, perhaps, is the crux of the matter and the clue to the eternal fascination of golf. The alluring nature of the game is that we can, whether by accident rather than design, execute a shot of such devastating brilliance that we visualize ourselves emulating the feat in a tournament like the Open Championship at St Andrews or even the Masters at Augusta.

Moreover, as weekend opponents, we maintain a competitive rivalry simply because golf possesses a handicap system, patterned to equalize our skills, which is the envy of all other sports. WS Gilbert wrote:

All shall equal be.
The Earl, the Marquis, and the Dook,
The Groom, the Butler, and the Cook,
The Aristocrat who banks with Coutts,
The Aristocrat who cleans the boots.

Golf has the ability to make all men equal. More importantly it has the ability to remind men and women of the values of life. You can stray out of eyeshot of an opponent, but if you choose to cheat, then the only person that you really short-change is yourself. The game was founded on integrity and that will live longer than any of us.

As Bobby Jones, whose achievements earlier this century can be pitted against those of Jack Nicklaus fifty years later, once said: 'Golf, in my view, is the most rewarding of games because it possesses a very definite value as molder or developer of character. The golfer very soon is made to realize that his most immediate, and perhaps his most potent, adversary is himself.'

All I need add is that, for me, golf is the most glamorous of all sports.

Mitchell Platts,
Great Missenden,
England, 1987

The Evolution of the Game

The origins of golf have been traced back to the Middle Ages and the name itself is said to derive from the Dutch word for club. Certainly by the fifteenth century the game had gained a loyal following in Scotland, and this aroused royal displeasure.

When King James II of Scotland, more than 500 years ago, saw his archers deeply engrossed in 'potting the ball' when they should have been sharpening their arrows to deal with the English invaders, he determined to put them – and the obsessive game of golf – out of bounds. He declared: 'That Fute-ball and Golfe be utterly cryit doune, and nocht usit.' And so a ban was entered upon the Parliamentary statute books in 1457 in order to break the hold that this game had upon his fighting men.

King James must have had a pretty good crystal ball to see ahead to the time when the game with a hole in it would become an obsession and an addictive influence with future generations.

This prohibition – like most others – would have its law breakers. That, of course, would ensure the survival of the game. Today golf's participants number millions around the globe, with television reaching an armchair audience of many more millions. Yet within the confines of individual golf clubs the game has, by tradition, an honorable estate of fellows with a masonic-like bond which few sports can claim – and many would like to emulate.

This, then, is the most honorable of games. It is one where you are expected to be as truthful and honest to yourself as you are to your opponent. How

LEFT: *Those who start young usually excel at their chosen profession. This young golf enthusiast of the sixteenth century holds a golf club which differs in shape from today's version. The ball is larger than the 1.68-inch ball in use today.*

RIGHT: *This artist's impression provides valuable evidence of a game resembling golf being played in the 14th century. It is taken from a manuscript in the Douce Collection.*

1384.—Golf, or Bandy-ball. (From a MS. in the Douce Collection.)

to play and score is based on trust. As a game of integrity and competitiveness played in a gentlemanly fashion it stands apart from those sports which rear temperamental followers and rivals. Of course its ups and downs bring out passionate feelings of disappointment in a player often critically directed at himself, but that in itself supercharges the challenge.

Many who view golf are both fascinated and mesmerized by the game in which a person knocks a small (1.68-inch) ball over distances of sometimes more than 500 yards in three or four blows. The same person can take the same number of strokes to hole out on a green in which a cup measuring 4¼ inches has been cut. In general if you play the game once then that is probably enough: you are hooked, dedicated whatever the cost, to achieve the goals of the game. With that comes the elation and the ecstasy.

There will always be some wrangle about the origin of golf. Who played it first? Who gave it to the world? There are a variety of contenders. Dutch old masters, for instance, show a game called *kolben* in a number of their paintings. Steven J H van Hengel, an acknowledged expert on the subject, had traced, before his untimely death, 'colf' back to 26 December 1297! Then the local townsfolk of Kronenburg commemorated the relieving of their castle one year earlier by playing a game not dissimilar to golf with targets, such as a kitchen door, rather than a hole. The French, Italians and Spaniards have rival claims. Stick and ball games abound, such as the Irish-Scottish pastime of shinty.

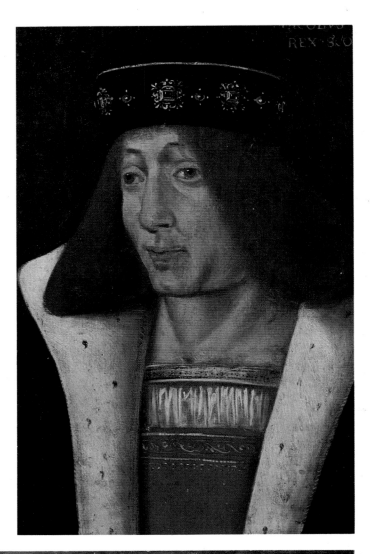

LEFT: *The Dutch old masters depicted golfers in the seventeenth century.* The Castle of Muiden in Winter, *painted in 1658 by Jan Beerstraaten, is a typical example.*

ABOVE LEFT: *Whether golf began in Holland or Scotland remains uncertain, although*

it is clear that King James II of Scotland (1439-60) banned his archers from playing the sport.

ABOVE: *Another Dutch painting depicting golfers:* Golfers on the Ice near Haarlem, *dated 1668, by Adriaen van de Velde.*

In fact almost anywhere in Europe you will find a historian claiming that golf originated in his country. There are documented details of the game in the Netherlands before the direct references attributed to Scotland in 1457.

Then there is a fifteenth century stained-glass window in England in Gloucester Cathedral, depicting a man swinging a club-stick implement. In some sense it is true to say that all of these stick and ball games contributed to spawning the Scots game.

We know for sure that the emergence of golf, as played today, was taking place over fields and scrub in Scotland when King James II put the ban on the statute book in 1457. So while there are various rival claims about the origins of golf, the Scots can rightly claim to have developed the game.

When James IV in 1502 sent off to his 'pro shop' for a set of 'tools' – a set of clubs and balls from his bowmaker in Perth – the Church soon showed interest in the game too. The then Archbishop of St

Andrews allowed players to tee off on the links although never on a Sunday which might interfere with the sermon! Failure to adhere to these regulations would meet with penalties, as John Henrie and Pat Rogie discovered to their cost in 1593. They were jailed for 'playing of the gowff on the links of Leith every Sabbath the time of the sermonses.'

By the middle of the eighteenth century golf was gaining in popularity. King James VI of Scotland had ascended the throne as King James I of England and in 1744 William St Clair, a hereditary Grand Master mason of Scotland, formed a golf club, the Gentleman Golfers of Leith, later called the Honourable Company of Edinburgh Golfers. This club would eventually move to Musselburgh and then to Muirfield. The Leith trophy was to be the first golfing trophy and would take the form of a silver club.

More importantly these 'Gentlemen of Leith' tabled the 13 rules of the Golf Manual which form the basis of those in operation today. Members were mainly masons who provided loyal support during the club's early years. In the United States too they laid the basic foundations of the game.

There, a Mr David Deas of Charleston, South Carolina, who had emigrated to America from Scotland, purchased Scottish clubs and balls in 1743 and began setting up a golf club. There is, however, no evidence that a club was established. Even so golf owes much to gentlemen such as David Deas.

LEFT: *Henry Callender in the uniform of the Blackheath Club, engraved by Ward (1812) following a painting by Lemuel Abbott.*

FAR LEFT: *James IV (1473-1513), who reigned from 1488 until his death, inspired interest in the game from the Church after he ordered a set of clubs and balls from his bowmaker – but the links were still out of bounds on a Sunday!*

RIGHT: *William St Clair of Roslin, painted here by Sir George Chalmers, caused the Old Course at St Andrews to be reduced to 18 holes because of his astonishing scoring exploits. He favored, as most of his contemporaries did, an exaggerated closed stance in order to give the feathery ball a firm strike.*

BELOW: *A view of the Brunsfield Golf Links in Edinburgh in 1806.*

ABOVE: *The game of golf was growing in popularity, as this illustration* The Golfers *(1847), depicting players at St Andrews, clearly shows.*

RIGHT: *The Swilcan Bridge at St Andrews in the 1850s, with 'Old Tom' Morris (far left), Allan Robertson (on bridge with a single club) and Major Boothby (about to play).*

FAR RIGHT: *William Inglis on Leith Links as the captain of the Honourable Company of Edinburgh Golfers. The painting, by David Allan, is dated 1787.*

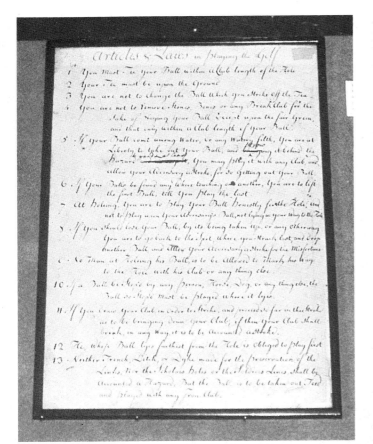

ABOVE: *The 'Articles & Laws on Playing the Golf,' enacted by the Honourable Company of Edinburgh Golfers in 1744, constituted the 13 original rules of the game.*

The implements (clubs) all had wooden shafts and heads, made almost solely in Scotland, and it was not until 1920 that metal shafts were produced. The canny Scots were soon exporting their golfing 'tools.' There are records of shipments to the United States around 1750, following that first consignment to Charleston, which suggests that golf was in the swing in other parts of America too.

Unlike today when players have matched sets with a system of numbering, the game then had its own traditional lore, with such clubs as the brassie, spoon, cleek (two or three iron), baffie, mashie (five iron) and niblick (eight or nine iron). Clubs like the wedge and putter were to follow later.

During these early days golf courses were often rough-and-ready affairs. The game could evolve around a piece of parkland or any piece of ground, provided one could pitch a ball and provided there was, say, a rabbit burrow to act as a hole. One of the first laid-out courses was that at Leith where the gentlemen would play with friends who shared their desire to find fresh 'greens' to conquer.

ABOVE: *A humorous sketch published in 1863 shows golfers enjoying an afternoon at Blackheath Golf Club.*

LEFT: *Another tournament unfolds at St Andrews, this one in 1859, with Mr Robert Chambers sinking a putt on the last green of the Old Course.*

ABOVE RIGHT: *The first tee at St Andrews in the 1880s.*

RIGHT: *Ben Sayers, the diminutive figure fifth from the left, became famous as a master clubmaker. He is pictured here at North Berwick on the shores near Edinburgh, which for some time, became one of the most fashionable golf resorts in Britain.*

Some would take the boat north from their new home at Musselburgh to a spot called St Andrews. Within a short space of time a club would be formed there. These 'links' close to the sea proved very popular, the short, weedy grass allowing the ball to run freely and smoothly. It was, of course, also easier to make contact with the ball in play. And there was the added advantage that there was less wear and tear on the clubs and the featheries – not inexpensive items.

These early balls or featheries, as they were called, were made of a stitched leather pouch which was stuffed with goose or other bird feathers, impounded very tightly into a small, sewn ball and waterproofed with a white lead-type paint. They were expensive to produce and subject to deterioration, so you couldn't afford to lose many of these. At first the implements were made of hazel or ash with heads of

blackthorn-beech or applewood. They were strong enough to withstand the rugged ground on which they would be swung. Later craftsmen developed these with varied angled heads into a combination of six woods and two irons to a set. As the number of clubs carried in the bag increased woods lost ground in popularity to irons.

How players dressed varied. Players who were not members of a club would play in their everyday clothing, wearing hats and coats which went right down to their hob-nailed boots. The more elite clubbers wore a sort of uniform and would be accompanied by their lads (caddies) who would carry under their arms the clubs of their master.

From these beginnings materialized the format of today's clubs. And when King William IV became patron of the Society of St Andrews he honored them with the title of the R and A – the Royal and Ancient Golf Club of St Andrews. In fact the Honourable Company at Edinburgh had appeared on the scene first. But it was the R and A that took charge. The club had been founded in 1754 when '22 Noblemen and Gentlemen, being admirers of the ancient and healthful exercise of the Golf' subscribed for a silver club to be played for annually. Even the silver club idea had been 'stolen' from the Honourable Company, as in 1744 the Edinburgh Town Council had presented the Company with a silver club as a prize for outstanding members. The Honourable Company, now based at Muirfield on the Firth of Forth to the east of Edinburgh, could boast a first when John Rattray won a club competition played over Leith's five-hole layout. Rattray became their first captain.

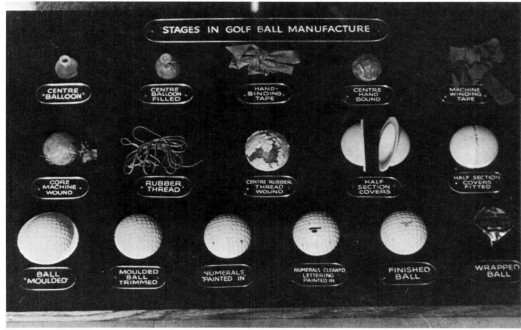

STAGES IN GOLF BALL MANUFACTURE

CENTRE 'BALLOON'   CENTRE BALLOON FILLED   HAND-BINDING TAPE   CENTRE HAND BOUND   MACHINE WINDING TAPE

CORE MACHINE WOUND   RUBBER THREAD   CENTRE RUBBER THREAD WOUND   HALF SECTION COVERS   HALF SECTION COVERS FITTED

BALL 'MOULDED'   MOULDED BALL TRIMMED   NUMERALS 'PAINTED IN'   NUMERALS CLEAN'D, LETTERING PAINTED IN   FINISHED BALL   WRAPPED BALL

ABOVE: *A display of golf balls, showing the various stages in the manufacture of early balls.*

TOP: *The refreshment barrow at the fourth – the 'ginger beer' hole – at St Andrews, with David 'Old Da' Anderson (center) serving beverages to P C Anderson (left) and 'Old Tom' Morris (right).*

TOP RIGHT: *Allan Robertson, considered the finest golfer of his day, ran a business manufacturing golf clubs and balls. He died in 1859, a year before the first Open Championship.*

It was St Andrews, however, that was to become the home of golf. Not surprisingly the Scots regard the city with enormous pride. It was at St Andrews, for instance, that William St Clair played a round in 1764 of 121 strokes and, because of his contemptuous treatment of the links, it was decided there and then to reduce the number of holes from 22 to 18. Thus it was that the Royal and Ancient became the ruling body when in 1834 King William IV conferred the title upon them.

Before this the early 'hackers' would play over common, links or scrubland on rudimentary courses consisting of a varied number of holes. The length between holes did not often vary a great deal in terms of individual distance. The shorter hole courses, however, would require a number of circuits. At some of these there would be up to 25 holes. Contests here were of match-play, with wagers struck on the outcome in head-to-head challenges and bets struck on the results at each hole.

Matches were sometimes organized by subscription: the competitor would agree to attend the ground and either pay dues to the club's 'messenger' or a sum of about a shilling which would cover the cost of food and drink too.

The match would start in those days with the ball teed up on a mound of earth or sand. The game would attract a gallery of ladies and gentlemen out for a stroll. Afterward the competitors would adjourn to the 'nineteenth' to partake of refreshments. Baillie Glass's and the Black Bull Tavern were popular haunts in St Andrews. And by all accounts there was ample consumption of liquid beverage with some individuals downing several bottles. There are stories then of the golfer, after the enjoyment of the day's play and the evening's socializing, taking himself off to bed with a measurable amount of his favorite tipple! When one considers that wagers were frequently struck in stakes of liquid assets it is no small wonder that they enjoyed their after-match activities.

Following St Andrews, clubs were formed more readily. Among these were Aberdeen and Crail on Scotland's east coast, and then others such as North Berwick. In 1851 Prestwick, which was to be the home of the first 12 Open Championships, was established. St Andrews, however, continued to take the lead and it was there in 1858 that the R and A framed a competition for a match over 18 holes. Allan Robertson, the accepted champion of the time, won, but with his death in 1859 there arose a question. Who would be the new champion? And where?

RIGHT: *Willie Park became the recipient of a big leather belt, presented by the Earl of Eglinton, when on 17 October 1860 he won the first Open Championship with a total of 174 at Prestwick. Park linked together rounds of 55, 59 and 60 on the 3799-yard course, which at that time had only 12 holes.*

BELOW: *A gutta-percha ball which was hand-hammered to improve its performance.*

BOTTOM: *A view of St Andrews.*

Willie Park and Prestwick, a small fishing village on the west coast of Scotland, would provide the answers. They would also transform the game. For the eight who pitched up at Prestwick's 12-hole course not only vied to be Robertson's successor but also introduced stroke-play as a form of competition. More importantly in 1860 the Open Championship had been born, although this had not occurred without a good deal of rancor.

The problem was that Major J O Fairlie, the Prestwick member who had proposed the competition, had invited professionals only. Many leading amateurs argued that it was unfair that they had been excluded and that it was not a true championship without their presence. In fact the competition had been arranged to determine Scotland's finest golfer. Even so Major Fairlie was compelled to announce that the 'Belt to be played for tomorrow and on all other occasions until it be otherwise resolved shall be open to all the world!' It remains so to this day.

So the 'half' Open was won on 17 October by Willie Park of the Musselburgh Club. He shot 174 for the 36 holes played – three rounds on the 12-hole course – with 'Old Tom' Morris finishing second. The prize was a red Moroccan leather belt with silver mountings, which was presented to Willie Park by the Earl of Eglinton.

By then the feathery had been overtaken by the new gutta-percha ball. This was a Malayan rubberized compound that served to give longer life and smoothness, although following its birth in 1848 it was to give way in 1870 to its offspring, the gutty, which incorporated cork and leather into the rubberized compound. Some credit the discovery of this new ball to a Dr Paterson of St Andrews. He had taken the rubber sole of his old shoe and had melted it to ply around the gutta-percha. However, its performance did not always match that of the old feathery. Experience promotes invention; as the smooth ball suffered knocks and chips as it was struck, so it was discovered, unintentionally, that pits and dimples would improve the performance of the ball. Indeed as the ball became more durable a hammer came to be used to indent its outer shell so as to obtain a better flight.

Britain's adventurous young men were now beginning to take their golf game with them to far-

RIGHT: *A photograph of 'Old Tom' Morris who, at the age of 40, won his first Open Championship in 1861, then returned to Prestwick 12 months later to successfully defend his title with a margin of 13 strokes – a record that still stands. He won again in 1864 and for a fourth time in 1867, by which time he had returned to St Andrews to become greenkeeper at the Royal and Ancient. 'Old Tom' held that position until 1903 and played in the Open until 1906. He died in 1908.*

flung parts of the world and forming their own golf clubs in these new regions. Exactly when golf was first played in the United States has never been clearly established, although there are a number of references to the game that date back to the beginning of the nineteenth century.

At Savannah there hangs an invitation dated 1811 to a golf club ball for a Miss Eliza Johnston. There is

BELOW: *A set of clubs used by the legendary 'Old Tom' Morris. These are his original championship clubs together with his tools for shaping the clubs and stuffing the balls.*

little doubt that there was a club in existence but there are no records to support the theory that golf was in fact played there. It *was* played in Yonkers, New York, by John Reid and some friends in 1888. He had asked a friend on a trip to Scotland to call in to the shop of 'Old Tom' Morris at St Andrews and purchase some equipment. Mr Reid, born in Dunfermline in 1840, had learned to play the game at Musselburgh. Now he developed a course, initially of three holes, which was to be called the St Andrew's Club of Yonkers on Hudson. At a similar time, maybe even a couple of years earlier, another club, Oakhurst, had been formed in West Virginia by Scottish settlers. However Reid, rightly or wrongly, is credited as being the 'Father of American Golf.'

Yonkers on Hudson later moved its course to an old apple orchard where members played over six holes and eager pioneers were to become known as The Apple Tree Gang. Club members there were also known for their habit of partaking of refreshments from picnic baskets at the final hole. At the Merion Golf Club today, instead of a pennant at the top of the flagstick, there is a small wicker basket that recalls the custom of those pioneering days of golf in the United States.

Early published versions of the qualifications needed to play the game which was, after all, a popular Scottish pastime, must surely have deterred many a would-be player. One early account gives the following detailed description:

The game requires much brawn and vigour. Accompanied by a servant (caddie) it requires men of exceptional physique, necessary to run to the full. His servant, carrying the required tools, follows and also clears the way ahead. Strong lungs, firm muscles of the legs and endless stamina are essential.

On an expanse of land holes are dug a foot or so deep and 4¼ inches in diameter. The holes should circumference the field at distances of up to 500 yards. The implements of the game comprise around ten types with a round ball of gutta-percha which should be painted white and weigh about two ounces so that it can enter the hole and be easily removed. The implements (clubs) are of various angled head shapes to lift the ball to where the holes are and to sink it into the hole itself. The reason for the variation of the angles of the tools is to suit the situation and distances the player finds himself in when he bats the ball.

The player starts from the first starting point and with accuracy aims towards the desired hole be it 100 or 500 yards away. Once the ball is in the air he runs forward – caddie following (with the rest of the tools) – and by luck or judgement aims to put the ball into the hole. Then he is off to the next hole, before his opponent. All the time his caddie attends his master, ready to hand the desired implement required for the next play. The said servant should be an expert in his selection of the tool for which ever the master's next play requires.

The player who is first to the hole holds preference whilst his opponent must wait until he has spooned the ball from the hole. The opponent then plays his turn whilst the first player plays off towards the next hole. This follows around the field and should the ball be put past the hole it must be knocked back until entering the hole. Should the other player distance his ball nearer the hole this gains him the ground.

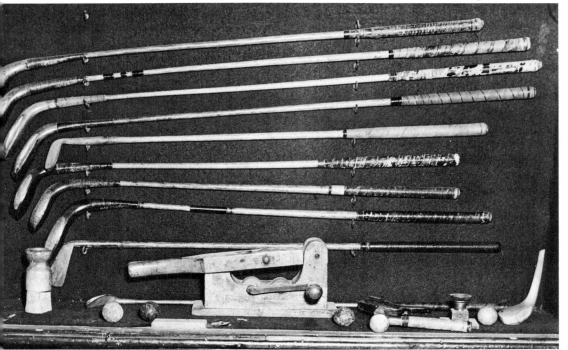

These observations may well have been a deterrent to a would-be aspiring American hoping to take up the game of golf. But in fact the United States would bring its own ingenuity of equipment and adjustments to the game of golf.

During these early days, when the game was really starting to take off, a spate of enterprising individuals cashed in on the game's sudden popularity in America (by 1900 there were more courses there than in Britain). Mr Tom Bendelow marked out a playing course within a day for a $25 charge. The course offered little more than a flat or circular piece of rough, patchy grass, but such was the increasing interest in the game that he, or his paymasters, had no difficulty in selling his services.

Charles Blair Macdonald was another colorful character. His knowledge of the game came from his years as a student at the St Andrews University. Big, bluff, self-opinionated, he was for all this a very good player – but not a good loser. After failing to win an invitation tournament which had been organized by the Newport Golf Club on Rhode Island in 1894, he ranted about how absurd it was to have a strokeplay in an Amateur Championship. One month later he was to lose again, albeit in the final, when the St Andrew's club agreed to play a match-play tournament. Old Mac, who on the final day drank a bottle of champagne as an antidote for a hangover, could still find excuses for his defeat. The result never made it into the record books. No doubt, however, some of this ranting and raving by a poor loser prompted some of the prominent golfing administrators of the leading clubs, of which Macdonald was one, to form in December 1894, the United States Golf Association. And who should become its very first amateur champion in 1895 – none other than one Charles Blair Macdonald. He was now to throw the full force of his influential and powerful personality behind the authoritative body.

The ten years leading up to the twentieth century saw American golf boom as 1000 courses were built. The best of these were credited to Macdonald's skills of planning, his Chicago course being a particularly fine example. High standards followed and many clubs flourished under the patronage of the wealthy. Most also had a Scottish professional who taught and supervised.

The first US Open at Newport, which took place in 1895, was won by an Englishman, Horace Rawlins. He had come over to work at the Newport Club and his scores of 91 and 82 were sufficient to beat off the others. His prize was $150. The following year he achieved second place to Jimmy Foulis, who was a Scot, at Shinnecock Hills.

One of the most important and significant items in golfing history was introduced around that time by an American. He was Coburn Haskell, an employee of the Goodrich Tire and Rubber Company, and he was responsible for the arrival of the rubber-cored ball. This new ball had its critics but it was essentially a watershed for golf. Basically elastic thread was wound, under extreme tension, around a rubber core which was then encased in a layer of gutta-percha. Confirmation of its excellence came at Royal Liverpool, otherwise known as Hoylake, in 1902 – one year

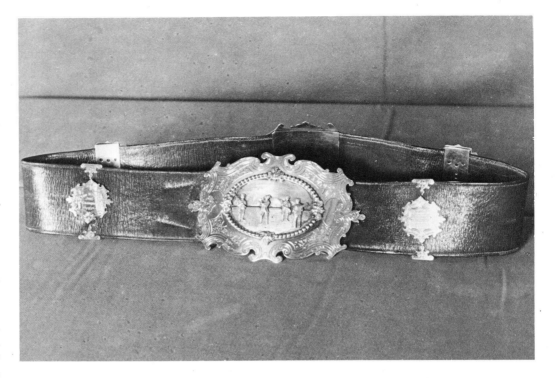

after its arrival – when Sandy Herd won the Open Championship. His achievement came after playing the same ball for all 72 holes – the Haskell ball! It was the end of the gutty and the start of a new era.

The Haskell ball was now appearing in British shops at a cost of two shillings. But it was soon to become the subject of controversy and scrutiny. The R and A and the USGA, the dual arbiters of the game, were together in agreement in 1920 that the ball should weigh no more than 1.62 ounces and should have a diameter of not less than 1.62 inches.

It was a different story eleven years later when the 'big ball' with a maximum weight of 1.55 ounces and a minimum size of 1.68 inches was introduced in the United States. Twelve months later the weight limit was increased to 1.62 ounces. The difference between 1.62 and 1.68 inches may not seem great, but Americans soon discovered that the bigger ball was easier to hit. It sat up more invitingly on the fairways and most found it easier to both chip and putt with. It took experimenting with the ball in the 1960s by the Professional Golfers' Association in Britain before the Royal and Ancient made the big ball compulsory in the Open Championship from 1974. Today the small ball is part of the past.

Clubs, too, had changed from the old hickory and persimmon types to laminates, composition and, more recently, metal heads. Because of the short supply of hickory the switch was made to steel shafts. The USGA cleared these for play in 1926 and the R and A followed four years later. In 1929 rustless chrome would extend the longevity of shafts.

The slight differences between the R and A and the USGA were all but erased when in 1950 the two governing bodies came together with a uniform set of rules for the game throughout the world. The R and A had laid down the original rules of golf back in the eighteenth century and in 1897 they had appointed a Rules of Golf Committee. America's USGA had also framed their own rules. Today the two august bodies renew the ruling from time to time and they provide joint decisions when asked to resolve important questions wherever golf is played.

ABOVE: *The Open Championship belt, first won in 1860 by Willie Park, was presented by Prestwick Golf Club, the host club, when the Open was inaugurated. The belt is made of red Moroccan leather and depicts golfing scenes on the silver clasp.*

BELOW: *The trouble with bunkers is that they always seem to get in the way. Here a group of golfers in the 1860s struggle to come to terms with a bunker at St Andrews.*

ABOVE: *By the 1880s women were enjoying the game of golf, although certain restrictions were imposed as to when they could play.*

The first club for women golfers was the North Devon Ladies Club of Westward Ho!, England, founded in 1868. At first women were restricted to the use of putters only – adopting the physical style of swing of the men was frowned upon! That didn't stop the determined golfers, however, and the sport began to blossom for them when in 1872 the London Scottish Ladies Club was formed. One of their members, a Mrs Pearson, formed a Ladies' Golf Union in 1893. There was no stopping the growth of the game. A British Women's Amateur Championship was played, albeit over nine holes, at Royal Lytham and St Annes, Lancashire, in 1893 and won by Lady Scott. She won it again for the next two years under match-play rules.

American women were quick to follow with their first official event being staged in 1895. Beatrice Heyt, at the age of 16, won the US Ladies' title in 1896. Like Lady Scott she won three times in succession and the women's game, like the men's, flourished. Competition between Great Britain and the United States was given a boost when Margaret and Harriot Curtis presented the Curtis Cup. In 1932 the Cup was awarded for the first time to the United States following the team's victory at Wentworth, Surrey.

The Curtis Cup is contested every other year like the men's counterparts – the Walker Cup, born in 1922, and the Ryder Cup, first played in 1927. Not until 1952 were British women to notch a victory although there was a more famous result in 1958 when for the first time they managed a half with the Americans on their own soil. That came after the era of Miss Joyce Wethered, later Lady Heathcoat Amory, whose classic swing, still regarded today as near perfection, was to earn for her a succession of one title after another.

In Glenna Collett the United States, too, produced an exceptionally talented player as she recorded six championship wins from 1922 to 1935. But America's first winner of the British Ladies' title did not come until 1947 when Miss Mildred Didrikson, better known as Mrs Babe Zaharias, took the title. She was followed the next year by Louise Suggs.

On both sides of the Atlantic, as the years rolled on, the great names of this glorious game etched their deeds into the history books. Names like Harry Vardon and Cecil Leitch, Bobby Jones and Patty Berg, Henry Cotton and Elizabeth Price, Ben Hogan and Mickey Wright, Tony Jacklin and Laura Davies, Jack Nicklaus and Nancy Lopez.

The men, assisted by others from around the globe like Peter Thomson of Australia, Gary Player of South Africa, and Severiano Ballesteros of Spain, had lit the blue touch paper. The women, too, craved to be part of the game as it exploded in popularity. Millions flocked to the fairways, magnetized by a game that was based on integrity, fired by invention and played by inspired individuals.

Golf Tees Off

LEFT: *'Old Tom' Morris, one of the pioneers of professional golf in Scotland.*

BELOW: *A golfing group caught in the rough in 1860. General Sir Hope Grant (fourth from left) watches, as does 'Old Tom' Morris (second from right), while Major J O Fairlie, who proposed that an Open Championship be played, prepares to hit.*

In 1860 the first Open Championship was played at Prestwick, a small fishing village on the west coast of Scotland. Organized by club secretary Major Jock Fairlie it was a competition between eight players to find a new champion following the death the previous year of Allan Robertson, considered at the time to be unbeatable.

Held over three rounds on a 12-hole course which measured some 3799 yards the championship was won by Willie Park of Musselburgh with a total of 174. Only one English club, Blackheath, acknowledged to be the oldest club 'south of the border' was represented. What Park's two-stroke win from 'Old

Tom' Morris did was to publicize the game to such an extent that three major English clubs were founded. These were Westward Ho! – or the Royal North Devon Golf Club as it is known today – the Liverpool Golf Club, later to be honored with the Royal prefix and known to many as Hoylake, and the London Scottish Club at Wimbledon.

Yet the 1860 event was not truly an Open. For no amateurs had been invited to take part although, following representation, this was rectified the following year in order to ensure its authenticity as an Open tournament. Park had put together rounds of 55, 59 and 60 in 1860. He was to score 54-54-59, seven shots better, twelve months later but he was still beaten by four shots as 'Old Tom' Morris handed in cards of 54, 56 and 53 for a total of 163.

Prestwick was celebrated as a course, its 12 holes spread over lofty sandhills. For the most part the holes were out of sight, so the golfer would experience a fascinating excitement as he lofted over the mountains of sand and clambered uphill to see how near the hole his ball had rolled. Or for that matter, how far away it was!

'Old Tom' Morris, however, was a master at Prestwick. He also won in 1862 and he recaptured the title in 1864 after Park had regained it. Born in St Andrews on 16 June 1821, Morris became apprenticed to Allan Robertson in the ball-making trade. He had in 1851 been taken to Prestwick by Major Fairlie, so he knew the course well, although in 1865, when Andrew Strath won, and when official scoring cards were issued for the first time, Morris returned to St Andrews where he was to hold the position as green-keeper to the Royal and Ancient until 1904. Willie Park won for a third time in 1866 but then back, once again, came Morris to take the title in 1867 for a fourth occasion. 'Old Tom' Morris had had his last win – but the red leather Championship belt would stay in the family for all time.

RIGHT: 'Young Tom' Morris wears the Open Championship belt which he won outright in 1870, so bringing the Championship to an abrupt end. The belt became his property, along with a princely first prize of £6. The Open was not played in 1871, but was revived in 1872 when 'Young Tom' won for a record fourth successive time. 'Young Tom' was recognized as a powerful striker of the ball and it is said that he broke many clubs with his practice waggle.

RIGHT: The monument to 'Tommy', son of 'Old Tom' Morris, was erected after contributions had been collected from 60 golfing societies. 'Young Tom' died of a broken heart following the untimely death of his wife.

For in 1868 'Young Tom' Morris, 'Old Tom's' son, scored a Championship best – 149 – for the first of three successive wins. In 1868 he set something of a record by scoring the first hole-in-one in the Championship. Yet he was to create a far bigger stir by winning the title again in 1869 and 1870. Under the rules the Belt, presented by the late Earl of Eglinton, became his property after his third win, and so in 1871 no Championship was held. It sparked an appeal which led to the members at Prestwick, St Andrews and Musselburgh raising funds for purchasing a cup for annual competition. The Open Championship was back to stay, although, unlike the Belt, it was deemed that the cup could never become the absolute property of one winner. The new trophy was a silver claret jug. It is still that today and the winner receives a replica. The staging of the Open was to be shared by those three clubs which had subscribed to the trophy that gave birth to the rota system.

With the move to St Andrews in 1873 the competition changed. There were now two rounds of 18 holes each, and Tom Kidd won that year with scores of 91 and 88. 'Young Tom' Morris was joint third and he was runner-up the following year to Mungo Park at Musselburgh. Sadly his days were numbered for in 1875 he died on Christmas Day at the age of 24 – he never fully recovered from the shock of his young wife's untimely death.

At the Open at St Andrews in 1876 trouble loomed. David Strath had tied with Bob Martin but there was a protest against Strath for playing his second shot to the 17th when there were still players on the green. Strath, annoyed at the objection and the committee's long-winded postmortem, stormed out and refused to take part in a play-off, with the result that Martin was declared the winner.

Jamie Anderson, born at St Andrews and regarded as the very embodiment of machine-like accuracy, won the title for the next three years and Bob Ferguson, a former caddie from Musselburgh, emulated him in 1880, 1881 and 1882. Thus Scottish golfers retained their grip on the Open Championship until in 1890 Mr John Ball Junior, whose father owned the Royal Hotel at Hoylake, became the first amateur to win the title. His credentials as a golfer of considerable ability were reaffirmed when, between 1888 and 1912, he won the Amateur Championship on no fewer than eight occasions.

The first Amateur Championship had taken place in 1885 at Royal Liverpool. It was not the success it should have been – invitations were sent only to certain clubs and an administrative faux pas resulted in there being three semifinalists! Thus A F MacFie received a bye at that stage and it was not until the Royal and Ancient took control of the event in 1920 that it was decided to recognize MacFie's win. This recognition also meant that the 1885 competition became regarded as the first. Bernard Darwin, authoritative writer, England international from 1902 to 1924 and captain of the R and A in 1934-35, captured it perfectly – MacFie became retrospectively canonized!

Following two successes by Horace G Hutchinson who was to become the first Englishman to captain the R and A, Ball won his first Amateur

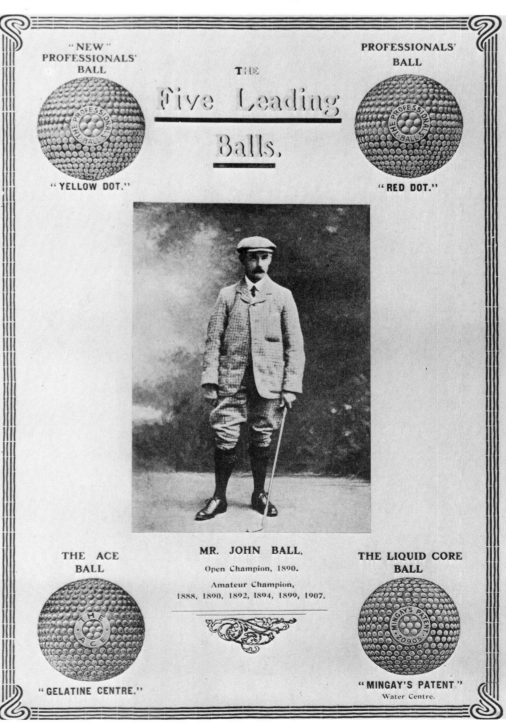

ABOVE: *Harold Hilton won the Open Championship in 1892, the year in which the Championship was extended to 72 holes, and again in 1897. In 1911 he became the first man and the only Briton to complete the double of the British and United States Amateur Championships.*

RIGHT: *John Ball shares with Harold Hilton and Bobby Jones the distinction of being the only amateurs to win the Open Championship.*

THE

"NEW" PROFESSIONALS' BALL

PROFESSIONALS' BALL

Five Leading

Balls.

"YELLOW DOT."

"RED DOT."

MR. JOHN BALL,

Open Champion, 1890.

Amateur Champion,
1888, 1890, 1892, 1894, 1899, 1907.

THE ACE BALL

THE LIQUID CORE BALL

"GELATINE CENTRE."

"MINGAY'S PATENT."
Water Centre.

ABOVE: *The Great Triumvirate of (from left to right) J H Taylor, James Braid and Harry Vardon, pose with Sandy Herd (right). Taylor, Braid and Vardon dominated the Open Championship from 1894 until 1914, although Herd managed to record a victory at Hoylake in 1902.*

TOP: *The Royal Birkdale Golf Club in 1910, showing the 18th green and the clubhouse.*

Championship in 1888. By winning both the Open Championship and the Amateur Championship he shares with Bobby Jones, who was to do so in 1930, the distinction of taking both titles in the same year.

Hugh Kirkaldy won the day again for the professionals in 1891. But in 1892, ironically when the prize fund soared from less than £30 to £110 and an entry fee was imposed, Harold Horsfall Hilton won. For the first time the Open was played over 72 holes and it was staged by the Honourable Company, not at Musselburgh but at their new home at Muirfield. Some observers expressed the belief that the 18 holes at Muirfield had a sameness about them which meant that they were not such a reliable test of golfing ability as the nine holes at Musselburgh. Hilton was to win the Open again, at Royal Liverpool in 1897, and in 1911 he became the only British player to hold both the Amateur Championship and the American equivalent at the same time.

Golf, and in particular British golf, was now to enjoy a golden age. The game would be dominated by three individuals known collectively as The Great Triumvirate – John Henry Taylor, a West countryman, Harry Vardon, a Channel Islander, and James Braid, a Scot. They dominated the Open Championship by chalking up a total of 16 wins between them in 21 years, and ruled the golfing scene until the First World War. In 1894 the Championship crossed south of the border for the first time to St George's, Sandwich, and there, appropriately, J H Taylor became the first English professional to win. He won again in 1895, 1900, 1909 and 1913. Harry Vardon, the Open champion record holder achieved six wins in 1896, 1898, 1899, 1903, 1911 and 1914, and James Braid triumphed with a succession of wins in 1901, 1905, 1906, 1908 and 1910.

The game had never known such giants even if 'Old Tom' and 'Young Tom' had held the winner's berth four times each. Vardon, the champion of champions, was born in Grouville, Jersey, in 1870. He set patterns and style of play that are practiced and copied today. His famous 'Vardon grip' – the little finger of the right hand overlaps the forefinger of the left – was not invented by him but he did popularize it. Today it is the accepted grip of most golfers even if Jack Nicklaus employs an interlocking grip – entwining the two fingers – and some, although this is rare, favor a double-handed 'baseball' grip. Vardon, like Taylor, was of average build and in keeping with this he liked to have a soft feel with the club. In essence he introduced the modern upright swing, bringing style, sweetness and accuracy to the game.

Vardon's consistency gave birth to tales of how he could make carbon-copy shots over two separate rounds, playing out the same divots as those of his previous rounds. The Vardon way certainly changed the way that golf was to be played.

LEFT: *The individualistic putting style of Harry Vardon is clearly shown to a large gathering of supporters as he coaxes the ball home during a challenge match against J H Taylor at Mundsley in August 1924.*

BELOW LEFT: *Golf was fast becoming a viable profession. Ted Ray (left) and Harry Vardon, the winner, are pictured at Sunningdale in October 1912, following the final of a £400 Professional Golf Tournament.*

BELOW RIGHT: *Harry Vardon won the Open Championship six times from 1896 to 1913. That remains a record for the man who put the 'Vardon grip' into the teaching manuals.*

LEFT: *Laurie Auchterlonie maintained the family's reputation in St Andrews, as master clubmakers, until his death in 1987.*

RIGHT: *J H Taylor in 1908.*

BELOW: *A scene during the Amateur Championship at Westward Ho!, Royal North Devon, in June 1912, where John Ball beat Abe Mitchell at the 38th in the final.*

ABOVE: *An impressive action shot of Harold Hilton taken in September 1911 when he won the Amateur Championship at Prestwick to complete his United States-British double.*

RIGHT: *John Ball drives during the Amateur Championship at Sandwich on 18 May 1914. This was not to be his year as he was beaten in the third round by H E Hambro at the 19th. Note that by this date the caddies had bags.*

Vardon had come to England from the island of Jersey in the Channel Islands so that he could gain more experience. He had been first a pageboy then a manservant and next an under-gardener. Now he was keen to follow in the footsteps of his brother Tom who was making a living from the game.

He took a job at Bury Golf Club, although he eventually moved on to Ganton. In 1893 at the age of 23 he entered his first Open. He finished one stroke ahead of his brother but 22 shots behind Willie Auchterlonie, who won with a set of seven clubs which he had made himself. Shortly afterward Auchterlonie was to found a famous club-making business in St Andrews where he had been born.

Golf, with its roots firmly in Scotland, had for the most part been played on the linksland – sandy coastal strips of what was virtually waste ground, formed after the last Ice Age when the seas withdrew, and where the raw, biting winds encouraged players to adopt a wide stance and hit the ball low. Vardon, however, adopted a different approach. He had a narrow stance and an upright swing. He would hit the ball high, imparting the kind of backspin on the ball that was foreign in his day and that led to the kind of precision which had seemed to be only a dream until that time.

Vardon, then, was to become very much a cult figure and one whose achievements would stand the test of time. Vardon, Taylor and Braid had all been born within 13 months of each other and it was Taylor who struck first in the Open Championship with his win in 1894. He retained the Championship twelve months later when at St Andrews he put together a last round of 78 – four shots better than anyone else had achieved that day – to win by four from Sandy Herd who had an 85.

Taylor, who lived until he was 92 and retired from golf only six years before that, did much to promote golf as a profession as well as to help found the Professional Golfers' Association. Indeed he did so much to raise the whole status of the professional golfer that Bernard Darwin wrote, 'He turned a feckless company into a self-respecting and respected body of men.'

Born at Northam in North Devon on 19 March 1871 Taylor had little education. He left school at eleven and he spent most of his formative days around the golf course at Westward Ho! in his native county. Unlike James Braid, Taylor was a small man with a quick temper. His craftsmanship as a clubmaker also earned him a high reputation but it is on his shot-making that he should be judged. A fine iron player, he was smart around the greens and deadly on them – as many of his defeated opponents found to their cost.

The start of his run of Open Championship wins was itself a part of history as he became the first English professional to take possession of the silver claret jug. The two other English winners prior to Taylor – Hilton and Ball – were both amateurs. His victory at St George's gave him great satisfaction but not as much as that at St Andrews in 1895 as he had vowed that he would win on Scottish soil. The historic and notable sequence of victories that The Great Triumvirate were to achieve had begun.

RIGHT: *Willie Park Junior, the son of Willie Park who won the first Open Championship in 1860, enjoyed his own success in the Championship at Prestwick in 1887 and at Musselburgh in 1889 when he beat Andrew Kirkaldy in a play-off.*

BELOW LEFT: *James Braid, who was a member of The Great Triumvirate, won the Open Championship in 1901, 1905, 1906, 1908 and 1910.*

BELOW RIGHT: *This sketch by Frank Reynolds shows James Braid (left) in 1910 during his fifth Open Championship which he won at St Andrews. Several of his contemporaries are shown too, including J H Taylor (bottom right) and Harry Vardon (center).*

The first of Taylor and Vardon's great head-to-head duels was to unfold at Muirfield in 1896. It was an exciting week, with the Honourable Company of Edinburgh Golfers receiving much praise for the changes they had made to the course since Hilton's win in 1892. On one day the wind was so light that it was insufficient to drive the windmill which supplied the clubhouse with water! Taylor led by three entering the final round but he shot 80 to Vardon's 77 and so the two great players went into a 36-hole play-off which Vardon won by four shots. Hilton returned to win in 1897 at Royal Liverpool but Vardon regained the trophy in 1898 when new regulations were enforced. It had been decided to implement what today is called the 'cut.' Any player 20 strokes or more behind the halfway leader was excluded from the final two rounds although there was the proviso that a minimum of 32 players should qualify for the latter stages. Vardon won by one shot from Willie Park Junior who had been champion in 1887 and 1889. In 1899 he won again, this time at St George's which boosted a record entry of 101 (albeit that many withdrew). Vardon cruised home by five shots ahead of Jack White who was to have his day in 1904. It was Taylor's turn again at St Andrews in 1900. Vardon,

who was runner-up, had been on tour to the United States where demand for his exhibitions kept him very busy. He did, however, find the time to go to Chicago that year for the US Open which he won.

Braid had finished third behind Taylor and Vardon in 1900. Twelve months later he finished first with Vardon second and Taylor third, so establishing The Great Triumvirate. Born at Elie, Fife, on 6 February 1870, Braid was a joiner by trade but he went to London in 1893 to work as a club-maker and he turned professional three years later.

It took Braid very little time to establish himself. He took part in a challenge match with Taylor in which they finished level. Next he teamed up with Sandy Herd in a £400 challenge match over four courses which was won by Taylor and Vardon. Even so Braid had by now proved himself a player of consistent merit.

Braid's record deserves examining. He was to win the Open on five occasions. He was runner-up four times, third twice and on no fewer than 15 occasions he finished among the top five. He also won the PGA match-play title five times, which reflects the strength of his game. In fact his temperament was perfect for such a frustrating game. His imperturbability was as

LEFT: Harry Vardon (sitting, left) and J H Taylor (sitting, right) in August 1908, with, behind them, Colonel Western (left) and A W Gamage (right).

BELOW: James Braid, five times Open champion, looks on as Cecil Leitch, then the queen of women's golf, gives a lesson in putting to the customers at Harrods, in March 1914.

RIGHT: *James Braid plays from a bunker at the second hole at Royal St George's, Sandwich, during the Open Championship in 1928 which was won by Walter Hagen.*

CENTER: *There are bunkers and bunkers, but the 'crater' at the 10th at Goswick, Berwick-upon-Tweed, presented a monumental challenge to those foolish or unfortunate enough to visit it.*

BOTTOM: *The 11th green at Ganton in 1913. Ganton was regarded as one of the most challenging courses in inland Britain at that time.*

important a quality as his powerful play. Even when there was every chance of driving into trouble he remained calm and composed on the fairways and it was said that 'nobody could be as wise as James Braid looked.' A modest man, he was one of the founder members of the Professional Golfers' Association.

Vardon came back to win in 1903, edging his brother Tom into second place at Prestwick, and that in itself was a minor miracle. His health had declined when in 1901 he had contracted tuberculosis. This had imposed some restrictions on his playing and was certainly instrumental in keeping him from winning more tournaments than he actually did for he was not to achieve his record total until much later.

For the moment it was Braid who dominated the scene. He won again in 1905 and 1906 and, after Arnaud Massy of France had at Royal Liverpool in 1907 become the first overseas winner of the Open Championship, he stormed home by no fewer than eight shots at Prestwick in 1908. Taylor bounced back in 1909 when for the first time the Open was staged at Royal Cinque Ports, Deal, but Braid was not to be deterred by this.

At St Andrews in 1910 Braid won for the fifth time in ten years. It was a remarkable achievement by this 6-foot 3-inch accomplished stylist who retained his game almost until his death at the age of 80. For on his 78th birthday he shot a 74. He continued playing competitively through to his sixties, never losing his touch. Braid was immensely popular – he was a jovial personality with an astute knowledge of and a passionate love for the game. A man who didn't mince his words he was regarded as a lively conversationist. People were drawn to him as a partner not only because he was a great golfer but because he was a person of intelligence and character.

ABOVE: *Arnaud Massy from France became the first player from overseas to win the Open Championship when he came home by two shots from J H Taylor at Hoylake, Royal Liverpool, in 1907. He had earlier taken a club-making job in Scotland, where he met and married a local girl, and he had subsequently become well versed in playing in British conditions. The next golfer from the continent of Europe to win the Open was Seve Ballesteros of Spain, in 1979.*

LEFT: *The Royal Liverpool clubhouse where Arnaud Massy achieved his historic win in 1907.*

 ABOVE: *Ted Ray, pipe in mouth, gave British golf a boost, at a time when the United States was beginning to dominate the game, by winning the US Open at Inverness, Ohio, in 1920.*

ABOVE RIGHT: *The crowd of spectators moves in as the 1924 Open Championship unfolds at Hoylake, Royal Liverpool. It was the turn there, once again for the colorful Walter Hagen of the United States to win.*

RIGHT: *James Braid at Walton Heath, Surrey, in 1927. Braid, who came from Fife, won all five of the Open Championships in which he competed.*

In 1911 Vardon again ascended the winner's podium at Royal St George's. He led comfortably at one stage but then he faltered and only just managed to tie with Massy, the Frenchman. Vardon, however, showed his dogged determination by overcoming Massy in the play-off. A popular win, yes, but a popular venue, no. The Open Championship, and the game of golf, were becoming increasingly popular, so much so that the accommodation in Sandwich had largely been snapped up by traders keen to do business there. This rather upset the players, as many had to stay at Deal which meant in those days a tricky journey morning and night on irregular trains, and it was implied by some observers that the state of affairs had led to much grumbling among the professionals.

Vardon, of course, went home to his club at South Herts, near London, supremely happy until beaten into second place the following year by Edward Ray at Muirfield. Ray had also been born in Jersey, though seven years later than Vardon, and his trademark was that he often played with a pipe clenched between his teeth. He could drive the ball a great distance and he also possessed great powers of recovery.

By 1913 Taylor was back, winning this time at Royal Liverpool. It was a fact that until then not one of The Great Triumvirate had won at Hoylake, although Taylor was to come home eight shots ahead of Ray, the defending champion.

Rejected by the army during World War I because of physical disabilities with his feet and eyes – the latter at times affected his judgment of play – Taylor might have established himself as the all-time record holder of the Open Championship. But along came Harry Vardon.

LEFT: *The Great Triumvirate of (left to right) Harry Vardon, J H Taylor and James Braid.*

RIGHT: *J H Taylor, who was still a formidable exponent of the game when pictured here in June 1923, finished down the field in this Championship which was won by Arthur Havers. The following year, however, Taylor finished fourth and in 1925 he finished joint sixth.*

BELOW: *In 1933 at Southport and Ainsdale, Lancashire, Great Britain beat the United States 6½-5½ to win the Ryder Cup for the second time. The Prince of Wales was present, and he is seen here (left of flag) congratulating J H Taylor, captain of the British team.*

The First World War was imminent and Taylor and Vardon, now with five wins apiece, had only one more chance before the Championship went into abeyance until 1920. It came at Prestwick in 1914 and Taylor did have his chance. He was two strokes ahead of Vardon moving into the final round. In his book *My Life's Work* Taylor admits, 'I do own to being a bit flustered when we got to the tee to begin the last round. The Glasgow trains had disgorged their hundreds of passengers, the crowd was large and insatiable in its desire to push forward and see everything that was going on.'

Taylor's putting, regarded then as perhaps the most consistent part of his game, let him down. He could not fight his way back after a seven at the fourth – Vardon took four – and his game suffered. Vardon finished with a 78 to Taylor's 83 and he won by three shots. It was a magnificent performance for it won him a record sixth Open Championship – a record which remains today although Tom Watson is poised to equal it after five wins himself.

So Vardon was, with his famous grip, able to grasp true immortality although an era of golf was, because of the war, to come to a natural conclusion. Braid,

Taylor and Vardon, The Great Triumvirate, returned to compete in the Open Championship following the war but they were no longer the force that they had been. The intervening years had not only removed some of their sharpness but the time gap had meant others had been able to improve.

The first player to take advantage of this opportunity was George Duncan. In one respect it seemed fair and proper as on many occasions before the war he had been compelled to play a supporting role to the Triumvirate. Now his chance came, although at first he was under some pressure after opening with successive rounds of 80. In fact he is the last Open champion to have won the title with a round of 80 or more during the week. His win came after he had finished in great style with scores of 71 and 72. It was an historic Championship, the first to be held under the auspices of the Royal and Ancient.

The six clubs that hosted the Open Championship decided that the time had arrived to have just one ruling body. So the R and A assumed responsibility, although this shift in power coincided with another that provided a pill far more bitter to swallow as far as British professionals were concerned.

In 1921 there was an historic United States win – albeit by a Scottish immigrant American called Jock Hutchison – and the cherished silver claret jug was winging, or rather sailing, its way across the Atlantic for the first time. In a play-off Hutchison beat Roger Wethered, the brother of that 'Lady of Swing,' the superb Joyce Wethered.

America's golfers were on the march. And in 1922 the first strident steps into the new dominance of golf were taken by the irrepressible Walter Hagen, a man of flamboyant character, with his Open Championship win at Royal St George's, Sandwich. It was to be his first of four Championship titles in eight years. Arthur Havers won in 1923, pushing Hagen into second place when for the first time the Open took place at Troon. But Britain failed to triumph again until Henry Cotton won in 1934.

In peacetime had been born a revolution. In the prewar years golfers like Taylor and Vardon had transported their game to the United States. They were regarded as world class and the only title that was thought to reflect their stature was the Open Championship. Now during the postwar years America would take the lead.

BELOW: *James Braid hands out cards on the first tee at Walton Heath, Surrey, before the start of the News of the World Match-Play tournament, in July 1945. This was the first big golfing event following the war.*

The Pendulum Swings

On 22 February 1888 John Reid invited several friends to his home in Yonkers, New York. One of them was Robert Lockhart. He was an immigrant Scot and, on a visit home, he had obtained a supply of golf clubs and balls. Meanwhile Reid, who also had Scottish roots – he was born in Dunfermline in 1840 and learned the game at Musselburgh – had laid out three rough holes in his pasture.

That day golf was born in the United States. The lunch guests had enjoyed the afternoon, experimenting with Lockhart's clubs, and they were to meet for dinner shortly afterward. Then and there they decided to found the St Andrew's Golf Club. Other clubs, too, came into being around that time and, although all elected to follow the rules of the Royal and Ancient Golf Club of St Andrews, each club conducted its own tournaments.

To most Americans it can be fairly assumed the pastime of hitting a ball, and of trying to pot it into a hole no bigger than a tin can, was nothing short of an insane exercise. Moreover the sport had no grounding whatsoever. For instance the US Amateur Championship was forced to change the date on which it took place in order to accommodate the America's Cup match at Newport, Rhode Island.

LEFT: *Walter J Travis, a late arrival to the game who only began playing at the age of 36 years, astonished the golfing world by making the Atlantic crossing from the United States in 1904 to win the Amateur Championship at Royal St George's, Sandwich that year. The 'Old Man,' as Travis was known, returned home to a hero's welcome.*

RIGHT: *Two young boys carry the clubs on the St Andrew's golf course in Yonkers, New York, in 1888, while (from left to right) Harry Holbrook, A Kinnan, John B Upham and John Reid practice their golf.*

RIGHT: *James Foulis won the US Open at Shinnecock Hills, Rhode Island, in 1896.*

RIGHT: *James Foulis won the US Open at Shinnecock Hills, Rhode Island, in 1896.*

BELOW: *In April 1903 the British magazine* The Illustrated Sporting and Dramatic News *noted that, while American golf was in its infancy, a certain Walter Travis was proving to be a golfer of high-class in America, and that 'It would indeed be interesting to see how he would fare when pitted against the cream of our own amateurs in the Championship here.' Travis won the Amateur Championship at Sandwich in 1904!*

The game of golf was on shaky ground not only because it was foreign to the nation but also because of the internal conflicts already raging between the few clubs that were then in existence in the United States. For both the St Andrew's and the Newport clubs had started competitions. Although good would eventually come from such difficulties with the formation of the United States Golf Association in 1894 these pioneers still faced enormous problems – best illustrated by the fact that Willie Dunn's name is excluded from most modern day record books dealing with the US Open.

Dunn, if he was alive today, would claim that in 1894 he became the first US Open champion. Dunn was small of stature – he stood only 5 feet 6 inches – but big in heart and his inventive skills are to be applauded. He was, later in life, to be one of the first players to experiment with steel shafts. He inserted thin steel rods in split cane and lancewood shafts. Moreover he invented a coneshaped paper tee – which would lead to the wooden tee – and later his pioneering efforts would lead to the introduction of indoor golf schools.

He had, in the early 1890s, met with socialite W K Vanderbilt. Vanderbilt invited Dunn to New York and so this dapper young man, with a penchant for wearing fedoras, joined a band of Scots whose experience and enthusiasm was to spark a greater interest in the game among Americans.

What happened, then, in 1894 was that the St Andrew's Club, which was staging its own competition, also decided to go one better – presumably to be one up on Newport – by simultaneously running an Open championship for the professionals. Dunn won the $100 first prize and a gold medal which he wore with pride for the rest of his life.

Sadly for Dunn, and perhaps this explains why he is often excluded from the record books, it was only later in 1894, on 22 December, that the United States Golf Association was formed. The rivalry between Newport and St Andrew's was clearly not good for the game of golf so together with representatives from the Country Club of Boston, Chicago and Shinnecock Hills they met in order to secure another American dream.

The formation of the USGA put new life into golf in America. Golf in the United States would make tremendous progress even if at first the US Open would be won mostly by immigrant Scots of mature ages. The 1895 winner was a 21-year-old Englishman called Horace Rawlins and the luckless Dunn filled the runner's-up berth. So today in most textbooks Rawlins' name heads the list of US Open winners.

Progress was swift – by 1900 there were 1000 courses – and in keeping with their promotional instinct, the adventurous Americans enticed Harry Vardon, already three times British Open champion, to the US for a series of exhibition matches. The establishment of the R and A had sired a lusty offspring in the form of the USGA. Vardon's tour brought the game to thousands of Americans and with the newly formed USGA getting into its stride the presence of this showman inspired many others to play the game.

Vardon spread the word of golf wherever he played. Everyone loves a winner and Vardon had the panache and style to attract big galleries of spectators. Even the New York Stock Exchange closed their doors early when Vardon was giving an exhibition locally to save the embarrassment of too many employees offering excuses for taking the day off.

Inbetween the exhibitions, when he was accompanied by his great friend and rival, J H Taylor, Vardon competed in the US Open at Chicago. He won and Taylor was runner-up. It was typical of the times but Americans were not slow in progressing. They learned fast simply by watching and appreciating the skills of master craftsmen like Vardon and Taylor.

After Vardon's win came the best of the Scottish settlers, Willie Anderson. He was a dour man from North Berwick and he shunned publicity. He could not but help put himself in the public limelight because of his rare talent. Just how big his talent was can be gauged by the fact that many observers believe that in any era he would have been a true champion. Records often speak louder than words and Anderson's four US Open wins have never been bettered although Bobby Jones, Ben Hogan and Jack Nicklaus would later all equal it.

Anderson won first in 1901. Laurie Auchterlonie interrupted his reign by taking the title in 1902 but Anderson won the next three. Anderson, too, did much for his profession. He was not amused when, just before the first round, an official at the Myopia Hunt Club in Hamilton, Massachusetts, in 1901, informed the players that amateurs could eat in the dining room but the professionals would have to go to the kitchen. Anderson, not one to lose his temper, roared, 'Na, na ... we're na goin' t' eat in the kitchen.' The outcome was that a tent was erected in which the professionals could eat. This was not entirely satisfactory but the professionals had at least climbed a couple of rungs up the social ladder.

In truth Americans, so keen to win, gave more of their time around the turn of the century to the amateurs. The reason, quite simply, was that there was a feeling that their amateurs could win whereas their professionals simply could not cope with the experienced British players. The surprise was that it took a player, who had only taken up the game at the age of 36, to produce the result that would send shock waves rolling through the British game. For Walter J Travis, an adopted son who had emigrated from Australia when he was six years old, crossed the Atlantic to win the British Amateur Championship in 1904 at Royal St George's, Sandwich.

Born in Maldon, Victoria on 10 January 1862, Travis was to leave Australia long before the formation of the Royal Melbourne Club in 1891 – probably the first concrete date for the start of golf in Australia, even if several previous efforts to start clubs had taken place both there and in New Zealand.

Even in the United States Travis was not taken by the game until, like many in that country, the end of the 1890s. He was, of course, a very late starter but he was unquestionably extremely talented. Proof of that came in 1900 when, at the age of 38 and only two years after he had taken up the game, Travis won the US Amateur Championship. He was to win again in 1901 and 1903.

Now it was time to take on the British on their own soil. Travis borrowed a center-shafted Schenectady putter from an American spectator and with that in his hands he proved unbeatable on the greens. He went past one opponent after another. In the final he faced Ted Blackwell, a hot favorite who could hit the ball the proverbial country mile. But Travis's putting power was more than a match for the powerhouse giant's advantage off the tee – Travis took Blackwell by the handsome margin of 4 and 3. This was almost tantamount to aggressive invasion. Walter was given a sour reception by the locals and the R and A even banned the center-shafted putter. That ban, of course, was later lifted.

Nevertheless an American had come to the old country, the birthplace of the game, and he was taking

home the Amateur title – the game of golf was the beneficiary. The 'Old Man' as Travis was nicknamed, returned to a hero's welcome and the United States rejoiced in the knowledge that they now possessed a true champion of the game. There was much more to come.

Anderson, sadly, was to lose his US Open crown in 1906 when Alex Smith won. He was on the way to an early death. His death certificate in 1910 recorded that he had died of arteriosclerosis, although others suggested that it was a case of acute alcoholism. Certainly professional golfers at that time were reputed to be heavy drinkers.

In that year of 1910, however, emerged one John McDermott who was to have a profound effect on the American scene. He was a cocky youngster from

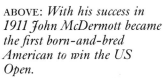
ABOVE: *With his success in 1911 John McDermott became the first born-and-bred American to win the US Open.*

ABOVE RIGHT: *Ted Ray, along with Harry Vardon, lost in a play-off for the US Open in 1913 to the amateur Francis Ouimet.*

Philadelphia who had risen from the caddie ranks with one fervent intention – he wanted to become the first homebred American to win the US Open. He was the son of a mailman and his desire and determination were reflected by the fact that he neither drank nor smoked. Indeed he rarely missed Sunday mass.

McDermott had to be content with a share of the runner's-up spoils in 1910 after he was beaten in a play-off by Alex Smith. His confidence, however, had increased to such an extent that early in 1911 he challenged fellow Philadelphian professionals to $1000 head-to-head matches. He won three in succession although all subsequent efforts to arrange another match failed!

In the 1911 Open it was McDermott's turn. This time, at the age of 19, he won a three-man play-off. Thus American golf had received the ultimate boost. The long wait was over. A born-and-bred American had won the US Open. It was all that was needed to give impetus to the growing flame, kindled by

Travis's Amateur Championship win in Sandwich, which would blaze a new-born hope of golfing glory across the length and breadth of America.

For now the game was as popular on the west coast as it was on the east. McDermott won again in 1912 and his two wins started a sequence when 'outsiders' simply were not allowed to win the US Open. Ted Ray did in 1920 but, that apart, it was not until Gary Player of South Africa took the title in 1965 that another overseas player won.

McDermott was tipped to complete the hat-trick at the Country Club, Brookline, Massachusetts, although there he faced the ultimate challenge. Harry Vardon was back for a second sponsored tour, this time organized by newspaper baron Lord Northcliffe. Along with Vardon came Ted Ray who had won the British Open in 1912 with Vardon runner-up. Vardon and Ray, who played with his pipe sticking out of his mouth, invariably attracted large audiences wherever they appeared.

But the tide of fortune was turning. While on that tour Ray and Vardon were to take in the US Open. McDermott was waiting for them but among the chasers there was also a 20-year-old local lad called Francis Ouimet and a teenage upstart from New York called Walter Hagen.

Ouimet's golfing education stemmed from playing on some rough holes carved in the backyard of his Boston home. Even so he had already indicated his prowess by reaching the semifinals of the US Amateur Championship. The kid, however, had ambition and as the Massachusetts champion he was quite prepared to take on such great players as McDermott, Ray and Vardon.

McDermott was not to figure this time but Ray and Vardon, each of whom led their qualifying sections, were there. They posted their scores of 304, leaving Ouimet at that time to play the last eight holes in one under par for a 79 to match the totals of the two British golfers. Ouimet heard a spectator talking about him: 'It's too bad but he's blown up,' he said. Ouimet was inspired by the remark. He vowed to himself and to his ten-year-old caddie, Eddie Lowery, that he would at least force his way into the play-off. He did so with a birdie at the 17th, holing from 15 feet, and a par at the last where he confidently holed from a distance of four feet.

LEFT: Francis Ouimet (left) and Bobby Jones arrive in London, following a transatlantic crossing, for the Walker Cup match at St Andrews in 1926.

BELOW: Francis Ouimet plays from a bunker during the Amateur Championship at Royal St George's, Sandwich. At the second round stage he bowed out, losing by two holes to HSB Tubbs.

ABOVE: *Outstanding golfer and popular personality, Walter Hagen plays from the 10th tee at Royal Troon during the 1923 Open Championship. Hagen finished runner-up, one shot behind Arthur Havers.*

The local hero and office clerk playing in his own backyard was taking on the formidable British pair in no uncertain style in a play-off which smacked of high drama. This unassuming youngster, an amateur, the epitome of American youth, seemed out of his class. Yet like a story from a boys' adventure book there had to be a magic ending. McDermott patted Ouimet on the back before the start, whispering 'You're hitting the ball well – now go out and play your own game,' and out Ouimet went in the misty rain with 10,000 spectators watching avidly.

Out he went, in fact, to make the tale come true. He overcame the famous British duo with a 72 to Vardon's 77 and Ray's 78. Vardon, it is said, was seen smoking a cigarette on the course for the first time in his career. Ray drew anxiously on his pipe throughout the game. Ouimet might have said to them afterward, 'Put that in your pipe and smoke it!' Instead, at the prize-giving he simply said 'Naturally it was always my hope to win out. I simply tried my best to keep this cup from going to our friends from across the water. I am very glad to have been the agency for keeping the cup in America.'

Sport, no less than any other activity, needs a hero. Better still if that hero has qualifications, like Ouimet's amateur status. Ouimet's victory was that of a small man overcoming the giants, the American Dream come true. There can be little doubt that this almost no-hoper fired the imagination of those who aspired to achieve against the odds. He had set

American golf onto the 'Fairways of Fortune.'

America would be roused into producing perhaps the finest exponents of this Scottish-born game, with others following the lead set first by Travis then McDermott and then Ouimet. Players of no mean ability were to come forward, possessing that little something else – personality and star quality. Walter Hagen fitted that bill to a tee. He was the streetwise kid from Rochester, New York, the indomitable predator of the fairways. Hagen would make bold predictions – and he delivered them.

Hagen had missed a chance in 1913 and had fallen by the wayside. At first he was against playing in 1914 at the Midlothian Country Club at Blue Island, Illinois. But a sponsor came in to pay Hagen's fare to Chicago. He took with him the same outfit that he had worn the previous year. It consisted of white flannels, with the cuff turned up just once, a loud striped silk shirt and a red bandanna which he knotted around his neck. He did leave behind the white buckskin shoes with rubber soles, because at Brookline he had slipped on the wet turf. Instead he wore shoes with hobnails protruding from the soles which offered extra grip just like spikes would later on.

That outfit said much for the man. And the dashing, flashing Walter won in style, too, with a score of 290. Between them McDermott, Ouimet and Hagen had sent the ball flying for American golf. They were men of exceptional character, charged with the desire to promote the game in the best interests of the

professional. Barred from using golf club changing rooms, they hired a limousine in which to change and in which to eat. Hagen, above all, helped to change that insensate outlook.

Ouimet was held in such high regard that the R and A bestowed upon him the exceptional honor in 1957 of appointing him the first non-British captain. He had visited Britain with Jerome Travers, another American amateur who won the US Open in 1915, to compete in the Amateur Championship after the war. So fancied were these two golfers that one daring individual wagered that one of the two would take the British title and he placed a bet of £10,000 at 3-1. However Ouimet and Travers would soon lose their position in the rankings.

Hagen was a very different character from Ouimet. But together the pair inspired more homebred winners, with Charles Evans Junior, another amateur, taking the US Open in 1916 before the war halted play in 1917 and 1918. But the irrepressible Hagen was back on the scene at Brae Burn, West Newton, Massachusetts, to win in 1919 following a play-off with Mike Brady.

The US title, perhaps fittingly, fell to Ted Ray, that old campaigner of the prewar days who had lost in the 1913 play-off to Ouimet, in 1920. He was, however, to be the last in the line of foreign winners until South Africa's Gary Player won in 1965.

By now golf in the United States was in full swing. There had been an air of indifference about the

ABOVE: *Walter Hagen and his wife celebrate his Open Championship victory at Hoylake in June 1924, to the amusement of onlookers.*

LEFT: *John G Anderson (left) and Jerome D Travers, the runner-up and winner respectively, of the US Amateur Championship in 1913.*

ABOVE: *Leo Diegel was the butt of Walter Hagen's humor at the Open Championship at Muirfield in 1929. Hagen, out partying the night before the last 36 holes, was informed that the leader, Diegel, was already tucked up in bed. 'Yeh, but he ain't sleepin',' replied Hagen. The winner? Hagen. Diegel had to be satisfied with third place.*

ABOVE RIGHT: *Tommy Armour receives the Open Championship trophy from Lord Airlie at Carnoustie in June 1931.*

RIGHT: *A young Tommy Armour, who was born in Britain before emigrating to the United States. He lost an eye during the First World War but later became one of the most authoritative teachers of the game.*

future of the sport. But the Roaring Twenties and the likes of Walter Hagen and Bobby Jones would alter all that. America was ready to launch into a period of expansion, the likes of which had never been seen before. That left the rest of the world behind as golf in the United States rode high on this bandwagon of euphoria.

The growing wealth of the nation, of course, was as much a spur as anything else. Henry Ford's legendary Model-T epitomized the foresight and inspiration among Americans. Along came the airplane with Amelia Earhart and Charles Lindbergh, and sporting stars such as baseball idol 'Babe' Ruth. The game of golf would share in this new surging, headlong advance.

The spirit of enterprise could be seen in the progress of club manufacture and equipment too. America immediately seized this opportunity to gain a large slice of the market. There was money to be made in clubs and balls. Interest in the game had risen to such a degree that the US Professional Golfers' Association had been formed in 1916 and with that had come the US PGA Championship. The US PGA first sprang to life following a lunch during which Rodman Wanamaker, the son of a Philadelphia department store owner, suggested to the party which consisted mostly of professionals, that the time was ripe for a US PGA Championship. The Championship started life as a match-play event, only changing from that format to strokeplay in 1958, and, of course, amateurs were not eligible.

Like most early competitions it would take a few years for an American champion to emerge. But in 1921 Walter Hagen won the first of his five PGA titles in seven years – a sequence broken only by Gene Sarazen's wins in 1922 and 1923. More importantly the US PGA Championship went to new courses, so spreading the gospel of golf, and there were new winners, like Leo Diegel in 1928 and 1929, Tommy Armour in 1930, Tom Creavy in 1931 and Olin Dutra in 1932, who would promote the competition.

But it was Hagen's impeccable performances in those years that did so much for the sport and for America. He was setting the pace in terms of appearance money in exhibition matches of such exhilarating style that his fellow professionals could have no qualms as the prize stakes for the tournaments grew.

Now, almost overnight, Hagen was to transport his skills to Britain. It was the start of the revolution. American golf had forged ahead to the point where it could directly challenge Britain. Now Hagen was to lead the way for a task force of Americans to monopolize the Open Championship. True, Arthur Havers won it in 1923 but Hagen scored again in 1924. Then came Jim Barnes (1925), Bobby Jones (1926, 1927 and 1930), Hagen again in 1928 and 1929, Tommy Armour in 1931, Gene Sarazen in 1932 and Denny Shute in 1933.

TOP LEFT: *Jim Barnes (left), winner of the Open Championship in 1925, waits to be presented with the trophy while the captain of the Prestwick Club delivers a speech.*

TOP RIGHT: *Jim Barnes recovers by the side of the 17th green at Prestwick on his way to his 1925 Open Championship success.*

FAR LEFT: *Gene Sarazen of the United States drives off from the first tee during the Open Championship at Hoylake, Royal Liverpool, in June 1924. Sarazen finished way down the field, behind Walter Hagen, but he was to win the title at Prince's, Sandwich, in 1932.*

LEFT: *Olin Dutra on his way to winning the US Open at Merion, Pennsylvania, in 1934, when he came from eight shots behind with 36 holes to play, to move past Gene Sarazen.*

RIGHT: *A team picture taken prior to the Open Championship at Muirfield in 1929 where Walter Hagen (front row, second from the left) won the trophy for the fourth time in eight years.*

BELOW: *Leo Diegel appeared to have a marvelous chance to win the Open Championship at Hoylake in 1930 but he lost his momentum from the 11th, where he is pictured, and Bobby Jones came through to win.*

LEFT: *From left to right are P E Leviton, Olin Dutra, Billy Burke, Walter Hagen and Al Free, at Gleneagles, Perthshire, prior to the Open at St Andrews in 1933.*

BELOW: *Walter Hagen leaves the last green at Muirfield, where he won the Open in 1929. He is congratulated by Henry Cotton.*

BOTTOM: *Walter Hagen escapes from a bunker.*

BELOW RIGHT: *A 1920s' advertisement – golf was becoming a popular pastime.*

Yet with his colorful personality and what he brought to the game, Hagen was to blow away some of the cobwebs of dullness and add the appeal that exists today. His bright golfing wear and lighthearted humor made him immensely popular and increased the galleries wherever he played.

Hagen might have crossed swords with official-dom more often than he cared to remember, but he roared throughout the Twenties. His butler would serve him champagne and oysters from the trunk of his chauffeur-driven limousine. Nicknamed 'The Haig' he would play in silk shirts with monograms and two-tone shoes. His trademarks, too, were hand-made suits and solid gold cuff links. He lived life to the full and he never forgot his own words, 'So many people today never have time to stop off and smell the flowers as they go through life.'

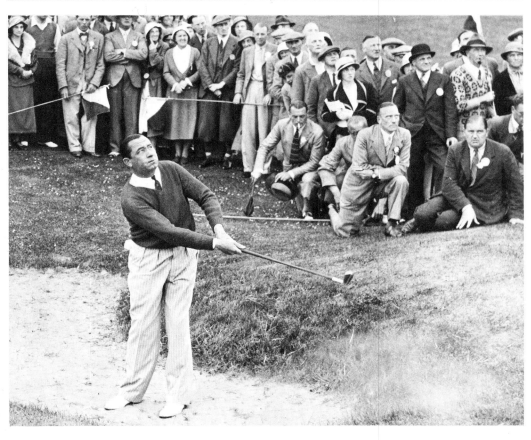

RIGHT: *Bobby Jones on his way to victory as an amateur in the Open Championship at Royal Lytham and St Annes in 1926.*

BELOW: *Bobby Jones drives from the 17th tee during the Open Championship at St Andrews in 1927 when he successfully defended his title with a record score of 285. He won by six shots from Aubrey Boomer and Fred Robson.*

The British, of course, were not too pleased with the annual loss of a piece of their sporting heritage. They were not exactly happy with this 'invasion' by American golfers and they frowned upon a certain R T Jones Junior who had the audacity to tear up his card at the short 11th in 1921 when he played in the Open Championship at St Andrews for the first time. Jones was to regret this rash act for years. Even so he was to be forgiven by the people of Britain, for Bobby Jones, as he is better known, not only learned from that incident but became arguably the greatest golfer in the history of the game.

Robert Tyre Jones was born in Atlanta, Georgia on 17 March 1902. The new breed of American Open champions in that rise of supremacy led first by McDermott, Ouimet and Hagen, and subsequently followed by Jim Barnes (1921) and Gene Sarazen (1922), was continued by Jones. Here was a man whose hallmark really was perfection.

Jones took little time in endearing himself to the public. His manner on and off the course was almost sufficient to persuade people in the United States and Britain alike to hand the trophies over to him. He could charm the ball with equal flair and his triple winning of the Open Championship in 1926, 1927 and 1930 should have been glory enough. His record included a memorable win in the US Open at Inwood, New York in 1923, following a play-off with Bobby Cruickshank. He was, of course, to crown his achievements in 1930 by completing the Grand Slam of golf, winning the US Open and the US Amateur and the British equivalents all within the same year.

Just for the record he shares with Ben Hogan, Jack Nicklaus and Willie Anderson the record of four US Open triumphs. He won his in 1923, 1926, 1929

and 1930 and he was was runner-up after play-offs against W MacFarlane in 1925 and Johnny Farrell (1928) and second, too, to Sarazen in 1922 and Cyril Walker in 1924. Jones was US Amateur champion in 1924, 1925, 1927, 1928 and 1930 apart from being runner-up in 1919 and 1926.

These are just a few of the major honors that Jones won. There was a great deal more to the man than simply these cups and trophies, and his achievements seem all the more impressive when one remembers the unlikely beginnings of his career. For instance Jones, or so it is claimed by some observers, was a weedy youngster with a shyness which had a self-destruct component. That apart, he had plenty of heart. And when his father, a lawyer, upped and moved home at the East Lake Country Club, young Bobby had the chance to prove himself. On that course – as at many others in America – there was a Scottish professional. In this case it was Stewart Maiden from Carnoustie, and Bobby spent many hours, days, weeks, at his side, using a trimmed shaft to develop the most natural of swings.

In truth Jones was able to reach the top because of his sheer measured talent. The road, undoubtedly, was tough, given the nature of the young man, but when he finally overcame his nervous unassured disposition it was to reach greatness of a level which, perhaps, in the history of the game only Jack Nicklaus can be said to have equaled. Yet it is a fact that Jones, a keen scholar who gained a first class honors degree in law, was such a nervous player that he was frequently physically sick during championships. With his stylish, rhythmical swing he was admired by all, but because of his nervousness he was still often unable to eat during championships.

BELOW: *The spectators at Coral Gables, Florida, are treated to an exhibition from a fabulous foursome: Bobby Jones, Gene Sarazen, Tommy Armour and Leo Diegel.*

Yet no one who knew the man would deny that in Bobby Jones was a person, a player, to inspire others. He had everything from ability to integrity to sportsmanship. If anyone ever ditched the theory about nice guys never making it then Robert Tyre Jones did and in no uncertain style. He was the one who raised the status of the US Open, making it the most important golfing tournament to win.

Jones had, in short, gained the love of everybody in the game. If an example is required then recall how in 1936, on his way to the Olympic Games, he stopped en route at St Andrews. There was not a soul in sight when Jones stood on the first tee, firing his opening drive down that wide expanse of fairway, nor was there as he approached the green. But the word was soon spread around the 'auld grey toon' that Bobby Jones was there. And by the second hole two thousand people had joined him! He was to return again in 1958, as the non-playing captain of the United States Eisenhower team, and St Andrews bestowed upon this much-loved man The Freedom of the Burgh. This was no lightweight honor since the last American previously accorded that distinction was none other than Benjamin Franklin.

Scotland never forgets its heroes. 'Wee Bobby's' popularity was legendary, and in 1927 he was carried off the last green after he had shot a record aggregate score of 285 – pushing Aubrey Boomer into second place – setting not only a new low for the Championship but a total in the Open for St Andrews which would stand until 1955. In 1958 Jones summed up his affection for St Andrews, saying, 'I could take out of my life everything except my experiences at St Andrews and I'd still have a rich, full life.' The whole assembly rose, in a spontaneous and emotional tribute, and sang to their dear, dear friend 'Wil ye n'a come back again?'

Jones, who died in 1971 after many years of suffering with a crippling spinal disease, had left his monument to the game. For it was back in Atlanta, after he had settled on a legal career, that he developed the idea of staging a tournament of his own. It was, of course, the US Masters and it has been played at Augusta, Georgia, since 1934.

Initially it took place in March to accommodate the newspaper sportswriters who were traveling home following the annual springtime pilgrimage to Florida for the start of the baseball season. Jones, following his Grand Slam in 1930, had retired at the age of 28. Business interests came first but, with golf in his blood, Jones wanted a place where he could play with his friends and he found it some 100 miles away from his Atlanta home. It was a nursery known as 'Fruitlands' and the 365 acres were for sale at Depression prices. The financing was not a problem because Jones had been befriended by Clifford Roberts, a New York investor who was quite willing to become involved as he, too, wanted a secluded place to play golf with his friends.

So, with the assistance of Dr Alister Mackenzie, a Scottish physician turned golf course architect, Jones and Roberts brought to life one of the great shrines of the game. They created a masterpiece at Augusta which became the perfect, permanent site for the US Masters. Jones, of course, had never visualized the

Masters becoming the important event it is today. That, however, is what the sportswriters of the time insisted on calling it.

Now the United States not only had the world's greatest golfers but also they had three great championships – the US Open, the US Masters and the US PGA Championship. The power of the British had sagged and it was now the turn of British players to go west in search of golfing greatness. Henry Cotton recalls, 'I thought that if I was ever going to be a good player I had better go to America and see just how they set about the game.'

It was an astonishing statement although one that could be supported by the results in the Open Championship alone. There had been twelve years of autonomous American control and it seemed destined to go on forever. Then in 1934 Cotton was rewarded for his thoughtful endeavors. He won the Open at Royal St George's. Britain had found a very worthy champion to end this dominance by the United States.

ABOVE: *Bobby Jones, who made his golfing debut at Merion in 1916, completed the Grand Slam there in 1930 when he won the US Amateur Championship. A plaque commemorates this achievement.*

ABOVE LEFT: *Bobby Jones (left) and Francis Ouimet study a score card following an amateur event in America in 1931.*

LEFT: *Bobby Jones (left) receives the Freedom of St Andrews in October 1958. He is pictured with the Provost R Leonard.*

FAR LEFT: *Bobby Jones retired in 1930 but he returned to competitive golf in 1934 in order to compete in the first US Masters on the course which he had built at Augusta. He teed off on 22 March 1934, and he took 76 shots to play 18 holes, but for Jones it was the playing, rather than the winning, that had by this time become more important to him.*

The Golden Years

In 1934 the inaugural US Masters was won by Horton Smith, the US Open by Olin Dutra, the US PGA Championship by Paul Runyan and the Open Championship by Henry Cotton. Two important milestones had been reached: the birth of the US Masters which was a watershed in American golf and Cotton's success at Royal St George's, Sandwich which would earn him the admiration of the British public.

That was natural enough since Britain had been starved of a home winner of their very own Open title for twelve years. Cotton opened with a 67 and he followed this with a record round of 65. That score was to give birth to a name – the Dunlop 65 golf ball – but more importantly it gave its maker a seven-shot lead. A third round of 72 stretched the advantage to nine.

Cotton was now home and dry, or so he thought.

The game of golf, however, is littered with stories of sudden U-turns by players psychologically destroyed by the special pressures associated with leadership. The slightest deviation from the norm can trigger a traumatic response. So it was for Cotton as, on reaching the first tee with five minutes, or so he thought, before the start of the final round, he was informed that there would be a 15-minute delay. The stewards required more time to organize the enormous crowd of spectators.

Cotton was totally unprepared for this delay. He sat alone in an empty tent with his stomach churning. It has been suggested that Cotton ate too much ice cream or spaghetti. Nothing could be farther from the truth. In those days two rounds were played in one day and, following his 72 in the morning, Cotton had sat down to a light lunch. It was sufficient to sustain him but as he was on a strict diet he did not over-indulge. The trouble for Cotton was that he had a delicate stomach and the delay simply activated his anxiety and this in turn brought on an excruciating stomach cramp.

He struggled to the turn in 40. Fortunately he had begun with an appreciable advantage and he managed to hole from 10 feet at the 13th to avoid marking a fourth successive five on his card. Cotton held on and the Open title remained in British hands.

Now Cotton, armed with the experience of touring America, could transform the game in Britain. However Hagen, responsible with Jones for turning the tide of fortune in America's favor during the twenties, would detonate Cotton's desire. On his 1928 trip to America Cotton began to realize that golf was indeed a golden game. Hagen was not only smelling the flowers but he was making a mint along the way, earning thousands from exhibition matches. Cotton would later recall: 'He was the man who made me think. I was impressed by his way of life and I wanted to be like him.'

The British scene, too, needed revitalizing. Cotton, a former public schoolboy, possessed the inspiration and the intelligence to do that. He was well versed in the eccentricities of the middle class. By demanding, and in many cases obtaining, increased prize funds he set new standards. He disturbed some officials, such as the French, by telling them in no uncertain terms that the only way to get the best players was to pay for them.

And Cotton was the best. Like it or not, his style, on and off the fairways, proved a winner. He could charm the birds from the trees. He became so celebrated that he was often invited to top the bill at certain theaters with a performance of trick shots. This, then, was the era in which Cotton dominated in Britain. He was to win the Open again in 1937, a victory in which there was much merit as many of the leading American golfers were present, and in 1948 following the Second World War.

FAR LEFT: *Horton Smith, a player much admired by Henry Cotton, won the inaugural US Masters in Augusta in 1934.*

BELOW LEFT: *Glory for Henry Cotton (right) at Royal St George's, where, following the victory in the Open Championship, he is presented with the trophy by Michael Scott, captain of the Sandwich Club.*

LEFT: *A large gallery watches as Percy Alliss putts out on the sixth green at Oxhey, Hertfordshire, during his fourth round match against C A Whitcombe in the 1936 News of the World Match-Play Tournament.*

BELOW: *Leonard Crawley, a fine golfer in his day, competes in the English Team Championship at Royal Birkdale in April 1939. Crawley recorded Great Britain's solitary point when they were beaten 8-1 by the American team in the Walker Cup of 1932 at Brookline, Massachusetts. With his approach to the last green he left his visiting mark – his ball struck the Walker Cup itself, denting the trophy.*

This was the time, too, of the Depression and it is fair to reflect that although Britain regained individual control of the Open leading up to the war years of 1939 to 1945, this was only because Americans suddenly turned their backs on the Championship. One could cite the cost of crossing the Atlantic as a reason, or the birth of the US Masters in 1934.

In fact there was no time clash, as the Masters was to be played in March, and then later on in April, and the Open in July but it did offer Americans another important championship in which to play. The great Depression might have been hanging over the United States but there was no stopping the expansion of golf. The Depression, however, had spread globally so that the British contingent at the first Masters was not exactly what Jones would have liked or expected.

The winner, however, was well known to Cotton. Horton Smith, a lanky lad from Missouri with imposing good looks, had won 11 of the 17 tournaments in which Cotton had played during his tour of America in the winter of 1928-29. It was an impressive record considering the presence of players like Tommy Armour, Craig Wood and Walter Hagen. Smith and Hagen, however, were like chalk and cheese, which showed in the different way they approached a game.

Smith would resist all temptations. He struck rigidly to a milk-drinking diet and he enjoyed nothing more than going to bed early. Cotton, in his book *This Game of Golf*, tells the story of how at one golf club function Smith sat next to a pretty, sophisticated woman who offered him a cigarette. Smith, a non-smoker, refused. 'Don't you drink either?' To that Smith replied 'No!' 'Then you have no vices?' came the next question. Smith, with a twinkle in his eye, said 'Oh yes, I have. I'm often short with my long putts!' As Cotton recalls about this incident, there was a lull in the conversation at that juncture.

ABOVE: *Following his success in the inaugurated US Masters in 1934, Horton Smith of Chicago receives the first prize check for $1500 from Colonel Robert T Jones, father of Bobby Jones.*

Smith was a superb putter and the marvelous greens which Jones built at Augusta National were made for him. He took full advantage by winning in 1934 and then again in 1936. The one nagging disappointment for Jones in 1934 had been the absence of Gene Sarazen. Sarazen had in 1933 won the US PGA Championship for a third time to add to his two US Opens and one British Open. He had subsequently committed himself to an exhibition tour through South America where the game had initially been transported by British golf enthusiasts employed to help build a railroad network in Argentina. The Buenos Aires Club had been formed in 1878, and with railroads encouraging travel and so spreading the golf bug, in 1890 another club was established at Sao Paulo, Brazil.

Sarazen was helping to promote the game although he had promised Jones, a close friend, that he would be at Augusta in 1935. At the time Sarazen was regarded as the leading player in the world, but not even this son of an immigrant carpenter from Italy could have predicted the stroke of brilliance he would execute in order to win the second US Masters. It was a stroke that would be marveled at around the world and which, unquestionably, put the US Masters firmly on the map.

Craig Wood, the runner-up the previous year, was back in the clubhouse with his score on the board. He had birdied the last hole and on hearing the roar of the crowd Walter Hagen, then 42 and Sarazen's partner that final round, turned to him and declared, 'I think we can say that it is all over now.' He knew that Sarazen would need three birdies in the last four holes to tie with Wood.

Sarazen was in the middle of the fairway at the 15th, a par five. As he pulled his fairway wood from the bag, ambitiously electing to go for the green guarded at the front by a creek, so Jones joined a dozen or so spectators near the putting green. The ball fizzed through the air. It caught the far bank of the water hazard but kicked on. It bounced a couple of times then, softly and to the amazement of those privileged to see it, toppled into the hole. Sarazen had made an albatross, or a double-eagle, and that alone was sufficient for him to tie with Wood. It was a winning blow in more ways than one. Wood, shattered by the shot, lost the play-off to Sarazen who had the psychological advantage. More importantly, the shot helped to breathe life into the game. The great Crash of 1929 had jolted the American population who needed their ambition to be rekindled. It was 1,000,000-1 shots like the one struck by Sarazen that helped to inspire them. Everybody needs a slice of good fortune in life and if it could happen on the fairways of Augusta then it could happen anywhere.

Smith too would enjoy a touch of luck in 1936 by holing a 50-foot chip during the final round at the 14th hole to give him his second victory. By then much was happening with the US Tour which had managed to survive the Depression. For instance in 1930 the St Paul Junior Chamber of Commerce had raised $10,000 in order to stage a tournament the week following the US Open. And Bob Harlow, who for years had managed the incomparable Walter Hagen, was charged with beefing up the image of the game to make it more attractive to sponsors and spectators alike. It was an Everest-like challenge in the sunken economic climate, but with the advent of steel shafts came better equipment and lower scores. It was easier to 'sell' an improving sport and players were now breaking 70 on a regular basis. That made better reading.

The US Tour incorporated approximately 15 tournaments with the leading money winner earning in the region of $7000. During the Depression, when one in four working adults were out of work, that, too, made pretty good reading. Even so not everyone was happy and that included George Jacobus who at the time was the President of the PGA of America.

Harlow was involved in promoting exhibitions in which players like Hagen whom he had managed, participated and he also had a syndicated golf column. In short there were clearly some people about who questioned Harlow's motives at times and some professionals who felt a certain section was receiving a rough deal. Jacobus grasped the nettle. He removed Harlow from the position of tournament manager and he also asked Horton Smith, a close friend of Harlow, to vacate his position as chairman of the tournament committee. Sparks flew with the appointment of Fred Corcoran, an Irishman who lived in Boston and was at the time working for the Massachusetts Golf Association.

Corcoran was paid a salary of $5000 and was

RIGHT: *Gene Sarazen, born in Harrison, New York, in February 1902, won the Open Championship in 1932. He returned to play in the 1973 Open Championship at Royal Troon, when the Royal and Ancient invited all the best champions of the past to compete, and he made an immediate impact by holing-in-one at the 'postage stamp' eighth hole. He was then 71 years old and it briefly put him on the leader board!*

BELOW: *Lawson Little of San Francisco, drives from the sixth tee at Royal Lytham and St Annes in 1935, on the way to overcoming Doctor William Tweddell by one hole to win the Amateur Championship for the second successive year.*

GENE SARAZEN

worth every cent. He transformed the scene by raising the prize fund in two years by $60,000 and in 1938 the professionals played a 20-strong tournament circuit for $160,000. In his efforts Corcoran was undoubtedly helped by the arrival of Sam Snead. The tour needed a breath of fresh air and Snead, from White Sulphur Springs, West Virginia, provided that from the moment he played his first practice round with four well-dressed, experienced professionals. Snead stood on the first tee in a long-sleeved white shirt and a pair of baggy pants. He hit his first two drives out of bounds, topped his next into a pond and, on being cajoled into reloading again, slammed his next effort onto the green – 345 yards away! So Snead, a bundle of fun and possessing the strength of an ox, became 'Slamming Sam.' And the Tour had a star to help to promote its wares.

Not that the 'old guard' had quite disappeared. Sarazen's crowning glory had come at Augusta in 1935, but in 1940 he was still on the scene when he was edged out in a play-off for the US Open at Canterbury, Ohio. His rival was Lawson Little and the tournament came no less than 18 years after Sarazen had won the Championship. Meanwhile Craig Wood, the man whom Sarazen had managed to destroy with his albatross two in the US Masters, eventually lost his unenviable tag as the 'nearly man' of golf.

A potted history of Wood's misfortunes would read like a killing field had all not come to a glorious end when through sheer determination he eventually triumphed. In describing his trials and tribulations it is worth recalling that in 1933 he finished third in the US Open then lost the Open Championship to compatriot Denny Shute following a 36-hole play-off at St Andrews. He was punished there by his big hitting, which on several occasions meant he drove himself into trouble, and it also put Wood on a run of more misses. He was runner-up in each of the first two US Masters. Another blow was dealt to him at the Park Country Club, Williamsville, New York in 1934 where he was beaten at the 38th hole by Paul Runyan in the final of the US PGA Championship.

Still the kicks kept coming. In the 1939 US Open

BELOW: Denny Shute fails to sink this putt during the US Open in 1929, but he did win the US PGA Championship in 1936 and 1937.

he tied both with Byron Nelson who had made his presence felt by winning the 1937 US Masters, and Denny Shute. Shute went out after the first of the two play-off rounds at the Philadelphia Country Club but Wood was still matching Nelson stroke for stroke after 36 holes. When they moved onto extra holes Nelson holed a full one iron – shades of Sarazen and Augusta 1935! Champions, however, never quit. And luck was about to change quite dramatically for this indefatigable character.

Wood had determined that the 1941 US Masters would be his, although his doubts must have been roused when after being five shots up he saw his lead being whittled away as Nelson swept to the turn in 33 compared to his own 38. This time his never-say-die attitude helped Wood to birdies at the 13th, 15th and

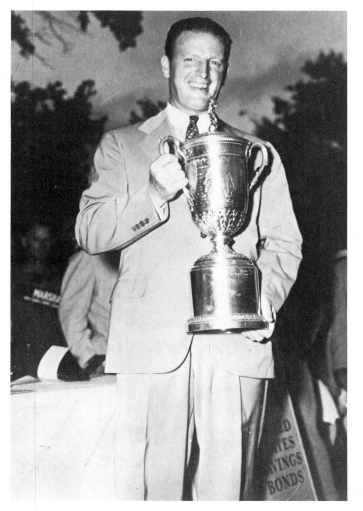

LEFT: *A smiling Craig Wood holds the US Open trophy in 1941 following his victory at the Colonial Country Club, Texas. Wood, who had a series of near misses in major championships, also won the US Masters that year.*

FAR LEFT: *Ralph Guldahl of Chicago, blasts out of a deep bunker on the 17th hole at Oakland Hills, Michigan, in 1937 on his way to victory in the US Open. He successfully retained the trophy 12 months later.*

BELOW: *Denny Shute of Worthington, Ohio, completes his swing during the US Open at Winged Foot, New York, in 1929, where Bobby Jones went on to beat Al Espinosa in a play-off.*

RIGHT: *Densmore Shute competing in the Catalina Open in the United States in 1929.*

FAR RIGHT ABOVE: *Lloyd Mangrum, minutes after holing a one-foot putt to overcome Byron Nelson and Vic Ghezzi to win the 1946 US Open, was caught in a heavy thunderstorm. Officials at Canterbury, Ohio, quickly provided Mangrum with a huge umbrella, while the large crowd cheered the 31-year-old from Los Angeles.*

FAR RIGHT BELOW: *Sam Snead recovers from the edge of a sand trap on his way to winning the 1949 United States PGA Championship at Hermitage in his home state of Virginia.*

16th holes, and he was home. Life's succession of ups and downs was at last turning for Craig in the kindest possible way. That same year he won the US Open at the Colonial Country Club in Fort Worth, Texas. Ironically he considered withdrawing on the eve of the Championship because of that most perennial of problems to a golfer – a bad back. Craig, however, strapped himself up and he battled to a three-stroke win over his old adversary, Denny Shute. The 'nearly man' had at last got there.

At this point the war intervened. The US Open would not be played again until 1946 when Lloyd Mangrum would emerge as the winner at the Canterbury Golf Club, Cleveland, Ohio. The US Masters, however, was played in 1942, with Byron Nelson winning, and that same year the US PGA Championship unfolded at the Seaview Country Club, Atlantic City, New Jersey, with Snead the winner.

Yet with the war ending, there was a new era dawning. This new era had been ushered in by Nelson and Snead and the tournament scene in the States flourished with the arrival, too, of Jimmy Demaret and Ben Hogan.

Samuel Jackson Snead, born in Hot Springs, Virginia on 27 May 1912, was destined never to win the US Open. He did, however, win the Open Championship at St Andrews in 1946. The United States had bypassed this, the oldest and most prestigious of championships, during the immediate prewar years. In addition to Cotton, Alf Perry (1935), Alf Padgham (1936), R A Whitcombe (1938) and Richard Burton (1939) had stepped in to win. More than 200 players, however, entered in 1946 and this proved the first real sign of the game's move toward becoming a truly international sport, for Bobby Locke of South Africa, and Norman von Nida of Australia, were among the many entrants.

Although Locke had played in Britain before, it was only after the war that he was to make his presence felt. Snead, however, was made the hot favorite and he won by four strokes, albeit with a little assistance from an official. Snead heard that one of his pitching clubs was likely to be singled out for inspection – the R and A had been told that certain American professionals were in the habit of roughing up the faces of their clubs – and so he asked a member of the Championship Committee for permission to use the club in question. It is said that he owed his homeward 35 to being able to use this club to stop the ball downwind on the lightning-fast greens.

ABOVE: *Byron Nelson competing in the 1955 Open Championship at St Andrews which was won by Australia's Peter Thomson. Nelson is pictured at the sixth hole during the first round on the Old Course.*

LEFT: *Byron Nelson at the 1939 US Open. He won after a play-off, setting an extraordinary record in 1945 when he won 18 of the 30 US Tour events he entered. He was runner-up in another seven and his lowest finish was ninth. That year his stroke average was 68.33 and he was 320 under par.*

RIGHT: *The US Masters Trophy can be viewed by anyone fortunate enough to obtain a ticket for Augusta.*

BELOW: *Sam Snead hones his game on the practice range in 1956 while watched by his son, Sam Junior.*

Snead, however, was a fine golfer and his record reflects that. He not only won both the US Masters (1949, 1952 and 1954) and US PGA Championship (1942, 1949 and 1951) on three occasions each but he is also credited with having scored no fewer than 135 victories. No less than 84 – a record – of those came on the US PGA Tour, his first being the 1936 Virginia closed event and his last the Greensboro Open in 1965. He did become a victim of the putting yips although he devised a unique method to conquer them. Originally he started to putt, croquet-style, between his legs but when that was banned he resorted to standing with both feet together, facing the hole and with the ball ahead of his right toe.

Byron Nelson, who became known as 'Mr Golf,' had an ideal golfing temperament. He was a methodical person with a good brain. His mechanical style is best illustrated by his record in 1945 when he won 11 consecutive events and a total of 18 in a single calendar year. For good measure he also won two US Masters, two US PGA Championships and one US Open. He was, however, to depart the scene early, seeking a quieter life because the high tension of professional golf did not suit his nervous stomach.

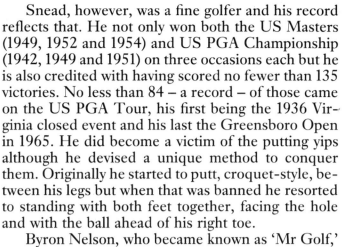

ABOVE: *Sam Snead displays his unique putting stance.*

LEFT: *Sam Snead on his way to being beaten in the singles by Harry Weetman, as the United States squeezed to a 6½-5½ success over Great Britain in the Ryder Cup at Wentworth, England in 1953.*

RIGHT: *Sam Snead concentrates on the ball.*

ABOVE: *Jimmy Demaret is regarded as one of the finest American golfers never to win a US Open. Demaret, who was born in Houston, Texas, won 31 American events during his career, including two US Masters.*

ABOVE RIGHT: *Henry Cotton drives from the fifth tee at Muirfield on his way to winning the Open Championship in 1948.*

RIGHT: *Henry Cotton coasted home by five shots in the 1948 Open Championship to win the trophy for the third time in his career.*

The likes of Jimmy Demaret, three times US Masters champion, galvanized the game. He was one of those gifted players who could sail along effortlessly without spending much time on the practice range. He had talent, sackfuls of the stuff, and a brilliant putting touch. He also had style. When he won his second US Masters in 1947 he dressed on Sunday like a canary with a bright yellow outfit. 'If you're going to be in the limelight then you might as well dress for it,' he said.

American golf, too, had come into the public limelight in 1947 when at the US Open at St Louis Country Club in Missouri a television camera was placed behind the 18th green. The prize fund that year was $10,000 – the first time a five-figure amount was at stake – but the presence of television, albeit just the one camera serving less than 1000 sets in St Louis, was to trigger a revolution. The message of golf would be relayed to watching millions because of a shot that owed as much to fortune as it did to skill.

George May, an eccentric millionaire, had backed a new event, the World Championship of Golf. The World, as it became known, grew in stature as the prize money increased, from $35,000 in 1949 to $75,000 in 1953. Lew Worsham, who had won the US Open in 1947, came to the last needing a birdie to tie with Chandler Harper, the 1950 US PGA champion. Instead those watching millions saw Harper scoop the $25,000 first prize, as well as some lucrative contracts, when he succeeded in holing a wedge shot for an unlikely eagle two.

ABOVE: *Ben Hogan, seriously injured in a car crash the previous February, shows that his swing is as smooth as ever as he practices during December 1949, prior to his comeback in the 1950 Los Angeles Open.*

LEFT: *Ben Hogan, who was partnered by Sam Snead, on his way to winning the Canada Cup (now the World Cup) for the United States at Wentworth, England, in June 1956.*

The public, coast to coast, were bewitched then, and again that summer by the presence of Ben Hogan at the Open Championship at Carnoustie. Here was a legendary figure whom some would consider to be the greatest golfer of all, although supporters of Jones and Nicklaus would argue with that.

Hogan had been a professional since 1931 but he had been around courses as an 11-year-old caddying at his home town club of Dublin, Texas. He had taken the top money spot on the US Tour in 1940 and, after the war years, he came back with a flourish by winning five tournaments in 1945.

However, he craved for the 'majors,' the title given to the US Masters, US Open, US PGA Championship and the Open Championship, and it was not until 1946 that he broke through into that league when he won the US PGA Championship by beating Ed Oliver 6 and 4 in the final at Portland, Oregon. Hogan was to win the PGA title again, whipping Mike

Turnesa 7 and 6 in the 1948 final at Norwood Hills, St Louis, and he eclipsed that with his victory in the US Open also that year at the Riviera Country Club in Los Angeles. Most observers regarded Hogan as the best in the world at that time – he had already been leading money winner on the Tour on four occasions and had taken the Vardon Trophy for the lowest scoring average no fewer than three times – but this victory was the final proof.

It could also have been Hogan's final input to the game and to life. He slumped into his Cadillac, exhausted by the ordeal of winning, and turned to his wife Valerie. 'Let's go home,' he said. 'I'm tired. I want to die an old man, not a young one.' So they set off to drive back to Fort Worth, Texas. The night was thick with a ghostly fog and as Hogan drove slowly into a small town called Van Horn he saw two head-lamps emerge from the darkness. It was too late. There was a sickening crash. Hogan flung his body across his wife, protecting her, and in so doing he almost certainly saved his own life. For afterward investigators found that the steering column had speared the driver's seat.

Yet Hogan would rally from his hospital bed, to usher in a new era in the history of golf. Some feared he would never walk again. Golf was out of the question. Hogan had a double fracture of the pelvis. He had broken his left ankle, his collarbone and just about every rib in his body. His left knee too was badly damaged. As Hogan lay on his back for two months so the sport appeared to have lost a hero in his prime.

Hogan, however, would not allow his injuries to deter him. He even posted his entry for the US Open in 1949. He did not make that event but he was, miraculously, at Merion in 1950. There Hogan displayed all the courageous fighting spirit that had helped to restore him to tournament golf.

He had tied with Lloyd Mangrum and George

Fazio and he would have to face another grueling 18 holes in the play-off after looking played-out at the end of the regulation 72. No sensible person would have dared to bet a dime against him, knowing the character of a man capable of picking himself up from such devastating circumstances, but the odds were surely stacked against him. Hogan not only won – he did so with a 69 to Mangrum's 73 and Fazio's 75.

This win provided the perfect recuperative medicine, injecting new life into Hogan's accident-battered frame. It seemed as though fate had rewarded a man's fight back against dire odds. Hogan was to win the US Masters and the US Open in 1951 and he repeated that double achievement in 1953. Next on the menu in 1953 for the galloping golfer was a taste of the British Open on the sun-baked links of Carnoustie. Hogan made no bones about his distaste for Carnoustie, with the fairways scarred by divot marks and the greens only improving as the rains came later in the week, but he delivered some tasty golf appreciated by every Scot who witnessed it.

He mastered the course, and at the age of 40 he won the Open Championship. Benjamin William Hogan, or 'Bantam Ben' as some called him, had played in his first and only Open. He had won three majors in one year and he might have completed what would become known as the Grand Slam if the US PGA Championship had not been held at the same time as the Open Championship. It had been a year of exemplary play. Yet Hogan belonged to that rare breed for whom there is always another summit to climb. He was the habitual trier. His comeback from that death-defying crash, and his impressive performances in 1953 probably provided him with a high point on which to retire. But the irrepressible golfer continued. Fate would, however, swing against him for he finished runner-up in the US Masters both in 1954 when he was beaten in a play-off by Sam Snead, and in 1955, and second in the US Open both in 1955 when he was edged out in a play-off by the virtually unknown Jack Fleck, and in 1956.

Hogan, who had at least emulated Sarazen by winning each of the four major championships at least once during his career, would make one final run for the US Open in 1960. But by this stage he had become a victim of the putting yips and he also faced competition from a man called Palmer who would revitalize the game on both sides of the Atlantic.

RIGHT: *Henry Cotton practices his bunker play prior to the 1953 Ryder Cup match when he was Great Britain's nonplaying captain.*

BELOW: *Lloyd Mangrum on the tee with a putter! The reason? Mangrum had overshot the 16th green at Carnoustie in 1953 and he was compelled to roll the ball back with his putter.*

Hogan's decision not to defend the Open Championship at Royal Birkdale in 1954 opened the door to a new champion. This time the up-and-coming kid was an Australian called Peter Thomson. He had turned professional in 1949 and because there were very few tournaments in his native country he came to play mostly in Britain where he charmed the spectators as a disciple of the basic fundamentals of the game. Thomson was to win three years in succession from 1954 – the first player to do so since Bob Ferguson in the 1880s – and once more in 1958 when he overcame the Welshman Dave Thomas in a 36-hole play-off at Royal Lytham and St Annes. Thomas's game was sound from tee to green, but his lack of authority on and around the putting surfaces proved his undoing, and he lost the play-off by four strokes, while Henry Cotton finished six shots behind Thomson and Thomas.

Thomson's spell was only broken in 1957 when at St Andrews Locke emerged from a state of semi-retirement to win his fourth Open Championship, following triumphs in 1949, 1950 and 1952, by finishing three shots in front of the Australian.

Locke had taken up the mantle following Cotton's last win in 1948 – Max Faulkner was to give Britain her last champion for 18 years with his success in 1951 – and like Thomson he was happier playing in Europe. He was christened 'Muffin Face' in America because of his changeless expression, but it was crossing swords with American officials that really hurt Locke. There is a theory that some Americans were put out when Locke scooped up dollars by winning six times in 1947 on the US Tour and then taking the lucrative Tam o'Shanter in 1950.

Locke nevertheless became a familiar figure in Britain and he and Thomson dominated the 1950s. Locke, skinny as a child, is best remembered as a portly figure striding across the fairways in a most

RIGHT: *Bobby Locke of South Africa putts out on the 18th hole at Royal St George's in 1949 to tie with Harry Bradshaw for the Open Championship. Locke went on to win the play-off.*

ABOVE: *Bobby Locke won no fewer than 80 tournaments around the world, including 15 in the United States.*

ABOVE LEFT: *Royal Birkdale, which is situated on a glorious stretch of dunes on the Lancashire coast, is recognized as one of the finest courses in Great Britain.*

LEFT: *Royal Lytham and St Annes, like Royal Birkdale on the Lancashire coast, was the scene in 1926 of Bobby Jones's first Open Championship win. The Open Championship also returned there in 1988.*

ABOVE: *Peter Thomson, watched by the crowd, escapes from a bunker at Hoylake during the 1956 Open Championship which he won.*

RIGHT: *Jimmy Demaret of the United States finds the going tough during the 1954 Open Championship at Royal Birkdale.*

leisurely manner, as if he was out for a walk, and he stood out too in his plus-fours, collar, tie and the famous white cap. He seemed remarkably serene at times, and his ice-cold putting technique would put the yips in his opponents.

Locke, however, seemed by accident rather than design to become involved in controversy. In 1949, the year of his first Open Championship win, he was to beat Harry Bradshaw of Ireland in a play-off at Royal St George's. Bradshaw, however, might have won that Championship but for an incident at the fifth hole in the second round. There he found his ball in a broken beer bottle. He could have taken a free drop but he elected to play the ball, even though this meant he might damage his eyes if the glass splintered. As luck would have it, the six that he marked on his card eventually made all the difference between winning and losing.

To beat Thomson in 1957, however, Locke had to survive a stewards' enquiry. On the last green Locke was asked by his Australian playing partner Bruce Crampton to mark his ball one clubhead's length away. He did so, some three feet from the hole, but when he replaced it Locke absent mindedly put it back where his marker now stood. It was an innocent error and the officials decided to take no action.

As Locke and Thomson dominated the British scene so the United States, in the wake of Snead and Hogan, produced a succession of fine players. Doug Ford had won the US PGA Championship in 1955 and the US Masters two years later. Cary Middlecoff won the US Masters in 1955 and the US Open twelve months later. Jackie Burke, the handsome Texan, completed a memorable double when in 1956 he won the US Masters followed by the US PGA Championship. Then came the incomparable Arnold Palmer who brought charisma as well as class to the game.

Golf was soaring toward the sixties, with prize money on the US Tour alone reaching an astonishing $1 million in 1958. The sport was obtaining more coverage on television, with even a weekly show called 'All Star Golf.' From coast to coast a growing number of people, both men and women, were watching the game. And with this heightened interest in golf some outstanding women players emerged.

LEFT: *Harry Weetman, suspended by the PGA following an incident during the 1957 Ryder Cup match, when he declared he would not play again under the captaincy of Dai Rees, remained in popular demand. Later that year he opened a new professionals' shop at Selsdon Park, Surrey, and he is seen here (second from left) advising Peter Waterman (third from left), then the British welterweight boxing champion, how not to hit a hook. Athletes Brian Shenton (left) and Gordon Pirie (right) look on.*

LEFT BELOW: *Peter Thomson, the defending champion, plays an iron shot at the 14th hole during the 1957 Open Championship at St Andrews which was won by Bobby Locke.*

BELOW: *A smiling Dai Rees holds the Ryder Cup trophy, following Great Britain's first win in 24 years. Behind Rees are Bernard Hunt (left) and Ken Bousfield. The American team was beaten 7½-4½ at Lindrick, Sheffield, in 1957.*

Women to the Fore

A rnold Palmer was to enrich the game in a manner that no other golfer of his time, or any other era, would emulate. A social revolution was taking place, on as well as off the fairways, and Palmer generated excitement as the traditional tweed look gave way to color co-ordinated outfits. His hitch-the-pants and go-for-broke style suited the swinging sixties. A man of daring deeds, he would become the darling of the fairways, influencing both men and women players.

Mark McCormack, a college chum, would see to it that Palmer's skills would revolutionize the sport. McCormack became Palmer's manager and he

LEFT: *Laura Davies, one of the many women golfers who have come to the fore in recent years. In 1986 she won the British Ladies' Open trophy which she holds here, a year after her triumph.*

RIGHT: *Catherine of Aragon first wife of Henry VIII, has been described as the first female advocate of the game. This illustration was drawn by Frederick Newenham and engraved by J W Knight.*

FAR RIGHT: *Mary Queen of Scots was a keen participant in golf although this was eventually to prove a considerable handicap to her. In 1567 she was spotted playing the game at Seton House soon after her husband's death, and that was used as evidence at her trial of her complicity in his demise. This miniature is by Nicholas Hilliard.*

would in time become the most powerful entrepreneur in the game, the agent for numerous sportsmen and sportswomen.

There can be no doubt that women have long been prominent in golf. Rosalynde Cossey, one of the leading authorities on the women's game, pinpoints Catherine of Aragon, the first wife of Henry VIII, as the earliest recorded female advocate of the sport. In 1513 while Henry was rampaging in France, Catherine, as governer of the realm, saw off the invading Scots and still had time to note that the game was in good shape: 'All his (Henry's) subjects be very glad I thank God to be busy with the Golfe for they take it for pastime; my heart is very good to it.'

ABOVE: *Women golfers in the grounds of Mr AW Gamage's Finchley Manor House in August 1908.*

RIGHT: *Isette Pearson, a member of the London Scottish Ladies' Club, displays the golfing gear of the time. Miss Pearson played an important role in the establishment of the Ladies' Golf Union in 1893.*

FAR RIGHT BELOW: *Miss Boyd in action at Portrush in 1911.*

NEW SILK :: SPORTS COATS

Registered design (*as sketch*), the most useful garment imaginable, beautifully made from rich quality, double-combed silk, extra bright finish, combining the fit of a perfectly made tailor coat with the comfort and warmth of a throw-on. A dainty and most becoming garment, stocked in more than 100 fashionable shades.

33	inches long,		63/-
36	,,	,,	72/6
44	,,	,,	94/6
Silk cap to match,			21/-

SENT ON APPROVAL.

Debenham & Freebody

Wigmore Street
(Cavendish Sq.), London, W.

Famous over a Century for Taste, for Quality, for Value.

ABOVE: *In this advertisement for a silk sports coat the model holds a golf club – a sign of the increasing popularity of the game among women at the turn of the century.*

ABOVE LEFT: *Cecil Leitch, four times winner of the British Women's Amateur Championship, plays, while Gladys Ravenscroft watches.*

The Scots undoubtedly lost a few good players at the Battle of Flodden that same year, but half a century and more later Mary Queen of Scots was roundly criticized after being spotted taking a gentle thwack or two 'on the playing fields outside Seton' only a couple of days after the murder of her husband, Darnley. Her reputation never really recovered.

It was another couple of hundred years before women further down the social scale took any real interest in the game but by the late eighteenth century the fishwives of Musselburgh, strong active people, were noted for their prowess, and they resolutely set about forming themselves into a society at their course near the city of Edinburgh.

In the early nineteenth century women also played at St Andrews but were generally frowned upon. And, according to Miss A M Stewart 'a damsel with even one modest putter in her hand was labelled a fast and almost disreputable person, definitely one to be avoided.'

It is all a far cry from the reception accorded the likes of Nancy Lopez and her colleagues nowadays even though prejudice lingers on. Any woman golfer hoping to play the top 100 courses in the United States as listed by the influential magazine *Golf Digest* would find that three of the courses are unashamedly banned to women players.

The female of the species has a stubborn streak, however, and will insist on playing despite the handicaps of dress, decorum and masculine derision. The St Andrews Ladies' Golf Club was formed in 1867, the first of its kind anywhere in the world, and the following year the Westward Ho! and North Devon Ladies' Club was founded in the southwest of England. There the only club allowed was a wooden putter, which made the advice of Horace Hutchinson, golfer and writer, seem irrelevant:

We venture to suggest 70 or 80 yards as the average limit of a drive advisedly; not because we doubt a lady's power to make a longer drive but because that cannot well be done without raising the club above the shoulder. Now we do not presume to dictate, but we must observe that the posture and gestures requisite for a full swing are not particularly graceful when the player is clad in female dress.

LEFT: *The prize presentation of the British Women's Amateur Championship in 1929 at St Andrews with (left to right) Glenna Collett, Doris Park, Mrs H Guedalla and Joyce Wethered (the winner).*

LEFT BELOW: *Joyce Wethered drives from the eighth tee during the Open Mixed Foursomes at Worplesdon, Surrey in October 1931.*

RIGHT: *A good gallery of spectators watches as the Women's Golf Championship unfolds at Royal Birkdale in 1935.*

BELOW: *Joyce Wethered plays from a bunker at the eighth hole during the 1931 Championship at Worplesdon.*

between 1906 and 1912. In 1905, they traveled to Britain for the Ladies' Championship at Cromer in Norfolk and they and the other Americans with them played a match against a side called England but containing several Scottish and Irish players.

'England' won 6-1 and the occasion was such a success that the Curtis sisters were keen to present a cup for future matches. They had their wish but it was not until 1932 that the Curtis Cup was officially instituted, with the United States beating Great Britain and Ireland at Wentworth in England. It was not until 1986 that a British and Irish side managed to win on American soil, overcoming not only their opponents at Prairie Dunes but also the alien conditions of a Kansas summer when temperatures soared to over 100 degrees Fahrenheit. Captained by Diane Bailey, it was the first golf team, male or female, amateur or professional, to succeed in defeating the Americans on their own soil.

Competing in that first Curtis Cup match were Joyce Wethered and Glenna Collett (Mrs E H Vare), two golfers who dominated their contemporaries and were undoubted giants of the game. In the top singles, the last match the two played against each other in major competition, Miss Wethered defeated Mrs Vare by 6 and 4, thus confirming her superiority.

In a classic encounter in the final of the British at St Andrews in 1929, Miss Wethered recovered from five down after 11 holes to beat Miss Collett (as she then was) at the 35th and win the title for the fourth time. Bobby Jones, who knew a thing or two, described Miss Wethered as the best player, man or woman, that he had ever encountered.

Glenna Collett failed to win a British title, losing in the final twice, but she more than compensated by winning the US Women's Amateur no fewer than six times – a record. She took over from Alexa Stirling, a childhood friend of Jones in Atlanta, Georgia as America's outstanding woman player. Miss Stirling won her native title three times in a row, in 1916, 1919 and 1920, with the First World War intervening in 1917 and 1918. Then Miss Collett made her debut.

Her forceful robust personality made her a formidable competitor; she won the first of her titles in 1922 and the last, under her married name, in 1935. In more recent times she has given her name to the Vare Trophy, which is awarded annually to the player with the lowest stroke average on the Ladies' Professional Golf Association tour.

Women professionals were thin on the ground in Mrs Vare's heyday, though in the mid-1930s Miss Wethered did forfeit her amateur status and traveled to America where she played a series of popular exhibition matches with the likes of Gene Sarazen and Babe Zaharias. Miss Wethered became Lady Heathcoat Amory not long afterward and was reinstated as an amateur after World War II, by which time she was devoting most of her energies to gardening.

'The Babe,' who had won two gold medals at the Olympic Games in 1932, was one of the great personalities of women's sport. She turned to golf with relish, establishing a reputation for fearsome hitting, even though she was by no stretch of the imagination a large woman. 'I just hitch up my girdle and let it rip,' she revealed when asked for the secret.

One shudders to think what Mr Hutchinson would make of someone like Laura Davies, the 1987 US Women's Open champion, who has been known to boom drives of 280 yards and more, delivering a healthy, uninhibited belt to the ball and worrying about the direction later.

Laura's forerunners set up the Ladies' Golf Union in 1893 and held the first British Amateur Championship that same year. It was won by Lady Margaret Scott, whose father had a course laid out in his private park. Thus advantaged, Lady Margaret won the title in 1894 and 1895 as well before retiring from the competitive game.

Over on the other side of the Atlantic the women's game was also beginning to take hold and the first United States Golf Association Women's Amateur Championship was played at the Meadow Brook Club, Hempstead, New York, on 9 November 1895. It was arranged at short notice and featured a mere 13 competitors, playing nine holes before lunch and nine holes after. The winner was Mrs Charles S Brown of the Shinnecock Hills Club, with a score of 132 – 69 for the first nine and 63 for the second.

In 1896 the championship became match play and Beatrix Hoyt of Shinnecock won the first of her three successive titles. She was aged 16. In 1900, at the age of 20, she gave up tournament golf.

The Curtis sisters, Margaret and Harriot, of the Essex Country Club, Manchester, Massachusetts, were a formidable presence in American golf at this time and between them won the Amateur four times

LEFT: *The Great Britain and Ireland team which drew 4½-4½ in the Curtis Cup match with the United States at Gleneagles, Scotland in 1936 are (left to right): Miss P Wade, Miss Pam Barton, Mrs A Holm, Miss B Newell, Mrs J B Walker, Miss J Anderson. Seated: Mrs P Jaron, Miss D E Chambers (captain) and Miss Wanda Morgan.*

RIGHT: *Babe Zaharias, outstanding golfer and athlete, at Wentworth in July 1951 during a tour by American women professional golfers in Britain.*

FAR RIGHT ABOVE: *Betsy Rawls of the United States tees off during the Open Tournament held at Wentworth in 1951.*

BELOW: *A team of British golfers who competed in a match against the United States Curtis Cup team at Sandy Lodge, Northwood, in June 1952.*

In 1935 she won the Texas Open and was then banned from playing in amateur events, only being reinstated in 1943. That opened the way for her to win the US Amateur in 1946 and the British title the following year, the first American to do so. She stunned the crowds at Gullane, near Edinburgh, not only with her golf but with her extrovert behavior. On the day of the final she appeared in red and white checked shorts which she was asked, firmly, to go back and change.

The Babe turned professional for good after that and picked up her first US Women's Open title in 1948, the year the Women's Professional Golf Association, founded four years earlier, foundered. 'It didn't collapse financially,' said Betty Hicks, a prime mover behind it, 'it just sort of faded away.'

In 1950 the WPGA's replacement, the Ladies' Professional Golf Association, was fully fledged and it was still flourishing more than 30 years later, with the 1987 tour worth nearly $11 million, a 21,000 percent increase from the early days. The pioneers were people like Betty Jameson, the first glamour girl of the tour; Peggy Kirk; Louise Suggs; Patty Berg; Marilyn Smith and Betsy Rawls, to mention but a few of the outstanding players.

The US Women's Open Championship was instituted in 1946 and was won by Miss Berg, who beat Miss Jameson by 5 and 4 in the final at the Spokane Country Club. The format was changed to strokeplay the next year and Miss Jameson won with 295, the first time, as far as anyone can ascertain, that 300 was bettered in a women's 72-hole tournament.

ABOVE: *Louise Suggs of Atlanta, Georgia won the US Amateur Championship in 1947 and the British equivalent the following year, before turning professional.*

ABOVE LEFT: *Patty Berg won the US Amateur Championship in 1938 and a total of 40 tournaments as an amateur before turning professional. She was the first woman to reach $100,000 in career winnings and she won no fewer than 80 tournaments as a professional.*

RIGHT: *Mickey Wright set a record for the United States LPGA Tour when in 1963 she won 13 titles. Her 82 successes on the US Tour remained a record until 1982 when it was beaten by Kathy Whitworth.*

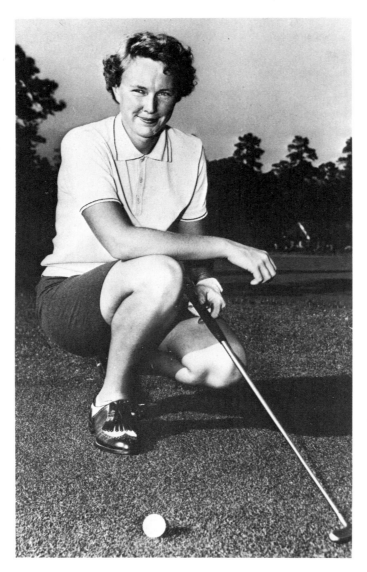

After that came the Babe who was runner-up in 1949, albeit a comprehensive 14 shots behind Miss Suggs. Her second title came in 1950 but it is her third victory that is most remembered, for it took place in 1954, a year after she had undergone surgery for cancer. At the Salem Country Club in Peabody, Massachusetts, her total of 291 was only three over par and left her 12 shots clear of the runner-up, Miss Hicks. The Babe never defended her title and died aged just 42 in September 1956.

Her successor as the dominant figure on the tour, in playing terms at least, was Mickey Wright (born Mary Kathryn), a quiet retiring woman who would deserve her place among the golfing greats. She turned professional in 1956 and gave due warning of what was to come by winning her first tournament, the Jacksonville Open. Over the next 13 years she was to win 81 events, including an unprecedented 13 major titles, and added an 82nd in 1973, four years after she had stopped playing regularly on the Tour. Only Kathy Whitworth has won more tournaments – 88 in all – but she would defer to Miss Wright in terms of ability and sheer class.

Miss Wright's accomplishments are legend and if she had been a more flamboyant personality, with even a touch of 'the Babe's' talent for publicity, she would certainly be better known as one of the superstars of the game. As a rule Miss Wright let her golf do the talking – though she did become the first player to be fined by the LPGA when she criticized the round-robin format of an event she failed to win, despite the fact that her scoring had been generally superior to that of the opposition.

RIGHT: *Mickey Wright blasts out of a sand trap near the second green during the third round of the Los Angeles Open at Inglewood in 1955.*

ABOVE: *Members of the 1976 Curtis Cup team.*

LEFT: *Pat Bradley from Westford, Massachusetts, turned professional in 1974 and won the US Open in 1981. Her record aggregate, achieved with a score of 279, brought her an extra $25,000 in winnings from the magazine* Golf Digest.

FAR LEFT: *Kathy Whitworth established a new record for the US Tour when she won her 83rd title in 1982.*

RIGHT: *Nancy Lopez became the darling of America's fairways in 1980.*

FAR RIGHT: *Nancy Lopez rejoices after sinking a long putt during the Colgate LPGA Championship at Sunningdale in August 1978.*

BELOW: *As she accumulated winnings of more than $1 million, so JoAnne Carner became recognized as one of the longest hitters in the women's game.*

Miss Wright won four US Open titles – a record shared by Betsy Rawls – four LPGA Championships, three Western Opens and two Titleholders' Championships, all components of the women's Grand Slam. She won three of the four majors on offer in 1961, a feat that was not matched until Pat Bradley, having her year of years, won a total of three out of four in 1986.

Miss Wright was one of the greatest streak players the game has ever known. Once she was in the groove she could win and win. In 1961 it was ten tournaments; in 1962 it was ten again, including four in a row; in 1963 she won four in a row again, amassing 13 in all; in 1964 she relented slightly and won only 11. In that four-year period, she came second 19 times and, hardly surprisingly, she admitted she felt invincible. 'It got to the point,' she said, 'where my swing was good enough that I felt I could not shoot a bad round. It was a feeling that stayed with me for four years.'

The trouble with that sort of dominance is that the moment you fail to win everyone clamors to know why. 'That gets to be more than you can handle,' reflected Miss Wright, who eventually suffered from what she described as 'emotional fatigue' because she was in contention week in, week out. 'It finally just wore me out,' she said. She was only in her mid-thirties when she stopped competing regularly and the LPGA player guide cites a variety of reasons including 'reaction to sunlight, aversion to flying and foot problems.'

A few years later in the mid-1970s the Tour itself was having problems. Prize money had risen to over $1 million but the LPGA was having trouble coping with its rapid expansion and was on the verge of bunkruptcy. In 1975 Ray Volpe was appointed as the first Commissioner of the LPGA and set about sorting things out. So successful was he that in his seven years with the Association prize money alone soared from $1.5 million to nearly $6.5 million.

Volpe's promotion of the women's Tour was given the boost it needed with the arrival of that rare, unpredictable, magical being – a superstar. Not just a good player but a good player who was delightful, charming, immensely attractive and full of life. Nancy Lopez had arrived, and the Tour had lift-off.

The public took to Nancy and her smile immediately and in her first full season on the Tour she won nine tournaments, including five in a row, eclipsing the feats of Mickey Wright and Kathy Whitworth, both of whom had won four. Television cameras recorded her every move while Miss Lopez was in Rochester, New York for the aptly named Bankers Trust Classic, the tournament that would give her the record. She did not disappoint, coming from three shots behind with a round to play, to win by two.

Her play may have impressed the fans – and they flocked to watch her – but it was her composure that impressed her fellow professionals. JoAnne Carner, no mean performer herself, with five US Amateur titles to her name and two US Opens, not to mention hordes of other honors, said of Nancy's performance, 'Nancy handled the pressure unbelievably. In fact, she seemed to thrive on it. For someone that young [Miss Lopez was 21] not to be overwhelmed was the most amazing thing.'

Miss Lopez proved her success was no fluke by winning eight tournaments the following year and topping the money list again. She was number one for the third time in 1985, winning a mere five times but silencing most of the critics who had said she would not last. Her swing, highly individualistic, contained at least ten faults, they said, and could not possibly stand the strain of a career on the Tour.

In 1987, having taken most of the previous year off to have her second child, Miss Lopez (by this time happily married to baseball star Ray Knight after an unsuccessful first marriage) won the second tournament of the season, the Sarasota Classic, to earn herself a place in the Hall of Fame, alongside the likes of

LEFT: *Julie Inkster studies the flight of her ball through the air. She won the American Ladies' Amateur Championship three years in succession, from 1980 to 1982. She later made a successful transition from amateur to professional.*

FAR LEFT: *Nancy Lopez in full flow.*

ABOVE: *Judy Rankin from St Louis, Missouri, was one of the fiercest competitors on the United States Tour during the 1970s.*

ABOVE RIGHT: *Ayako Okamoto became in 1982 only the second Japanese golfer to win on the United States LPGA circuit when she won the Arizona Copper Classic.*

RIGHT: *Australia's Jan Stephenson is regarded as the glamour girl of the fairways.*

Berg, Zaharias, Wright and Carner. It is an exclusive club, with only 11 women members to date and Miss Lopez was inducted with due pomp and ceremony in the glittering setting of Tiffany's on Fifth Avenue.

If there is one glaring gap in Miss Lopez's record it is that she has not won the US Women's Open. This is not an omission that figures in the career of Laura Davies, the tall, blond Englishwoman who may well take the LPGA tour by storm in the next few years. The leading player on the young but improving WPGA tour in Europe, Laura Davies was more or less unheralded when she arrived in Plainfield, New Jersey, for the 1987 Open, though a few people knew of her reputation for long hitting.

By the end of the extended championship – it lasted six days because of a thunderstorm and a play-off – she had become a celebrity and won the title. She defeated JoAnne Carner as well as Ayako Okamoto of Japan (who all season had been vying with Betsy King and Jane Geddes at the top of the money list) in an 18-hole play-off, leaving them slightly bemused by her enormous power and immense calm – and mightily impressed by her talent.

Miss Davies's intention had been to attend the LPGA's qualifying events in a bid to earn her card for 1988 but the Association had the good sense to change its rules and exempt her from qualifying. Any non-LPGA member who won one of the tour's domestic events would be eligible to compete the following season without the formality of qualifying.

The situation had not arisen before because of the three previous foreign winners of the Open, Fay Crocker, a Uruguayan, was an LPGA member, as was Jan Stephenson, the glamorous Australian, and the remarkable Catherine Lacoste of France was an amateur. Miss Lacoste was 22 years and five days old when she won the title in 1967 and remains the youngest champion ever, as well as the only amateur winner. Two years later, she won both the British Amateur and the US Amateur titles, following Dorothy Campbell (1909) and Pam Barton (1936) as the third person to achieve that particular double.

ABOVE: *With her success in 1987 Laura Davies became the first British golfer to win the United States Open.*

RIGHT: *Betsy King turned professional in 1977; in recent years she has become a consistent money winner.*

FAR RIGHT: *Catherine Lacoste of France won the US Women's Open as an amateur in 1967.*

RIGHT: *Abe Mitchell by the edge of the stream during the Amateur Championship at Westwood Ho! in 1912.*

The day of the great amateur would die with the advent of professional golf as we know it today. Clearly the rewards have become so great that there is no incentive for the budding Bobby Joneses to remain attached to the amateur ranks. That is not a criticism, rather a statement of fact, and the world of golf would most certainly be emptier without some of the outstanding amateurs who have graced the fairways. Nobody, for instance, will ever equal the achievement of John Ball in winning the British Amateur no fewer than eight times, the last occasion being at Westward Ho! with his success in 1912.

Ball's brilliant performances took place before Americans began to compete regularly in the Amateur Championship with the inauguration of the Walker Cup. That match began on the eve of the Amateur Championship at Royal Liverpool in 1921, although the first official encounter between Great Britain and Ireland and the United States did not take place until the following year. It came about following a rules meeting between the Royal and Ancient and the United States Golf Association at which George Herbert Walker of the National Links of America was present in his capacity as the President of the USGA.

LEFT: *Bobby Jones on his way to winning the American Championship at St Andrews in 1930.*

LEFT: *The Walker Cup, inaugurated in 1922, began a series of amateur confrontations between the United States and Great Britain & Ireland.*

TOP: *Bobby Jones (playing) beats Roger Wethered 9 and 8 as the United States beat Great Britain in the Walker Cup at Sandwich in 1930.*

ABOVE: *Bobby Jones (seated, left), the nonplaying captain of the United States team, is seen here with the Australian team winners of the 1958 Eisenhower Trophy at St Andrews.*

RIGHT: *Charles Coe, the captain, and his team-mate Harvie Ward, hold the Walker Cup once again following America's victory at Muirfield in 1959.*

Walker, fired by the suggestion of a regular fixture between the nations, offered a trophy, and with a little assistance from various newspapers the match became known as the Walker Cup. Initially the tournament was played annually but like the Ryder Cup, the professional counterpart, it subsequently became a biennial affair following the 1924 contest during which it was pointed out that a meeting every other year might help the longevity of the match.

When the teams did meet again in 1926, with Bobby Jones beating Cyril Tolley 12 and 11 as the Americans squeezed to a narrow win, it was clear that the golfers from the United States were establishing a supremacy in a sport initially popularized by the British nation. Jess Sweetner, for instance, was to win the Amateur Championship in 1926 and so start a trend, with Americans winning consistently in Walker Cup years in Britain right up until 1963 when Michael Lunt broke the spell.

It is the US Amateur Championship, however, of 1930 which lives longest in the memory of golfing historians. For it was that year at Merion that the Grand Slam dream of Bobby Jones came to fruition as he beat Eugene Homans 8 and 7 to complete his unprecedented four-timer. Jones had won the British and US Opens and the British and US Amateur Championships. The US Amateur in 1930 was to be his last championship.

Even so twelve months later the US Amateur was again to become headline news. What could one say as Francis Ouimet, the hero of the 1913 US Open, followed Jones by winning the 1931 US Amateur title – 17 years after his first win in 1914. The irony is that Jack Westland, whom Ouimet defeated in that final, was himself to create a record in 1952 by winning the championship at the age of 48 to become the oldest champion.

As time progressed so the US Amateur champions led by the likes of Arnold Palmer and Jack Nicklaus, the winners in 1954 and 1959 respectively, would become familiar names in the professional world. Palmer, however, turned professional shortly afterward whereas Nicklaus waited until 1961 when he overcame Dudley Wysong 8 and 6 in the final to win again at Pebble Beach.

Even so it was not until the 1970s that the US Amateur champions became recognized for making a successful transition to the professional ranks. Lanny Wadkins (1970), Craig Stadler (1973), Jerry Pate (1974), John Cook (1978), Mark O'Meara (1979) and Hal Sutton (1980) were to change the trend.

The same, perhaps, cannot be said of the British Amateur, except perhaps for the success of Jose-Maria Olazabal of Spain in 1984. His star moved into ascendancy with that sparkling triumph and it also illuminated the increasing influence that players from the European continent would have on the game of golf. That influence has shown itself in the Ryder Cup, with the inclusion of continental players and victories over the United States, but in the Walker Cup there remains a strictly Great Britain and Ireland team. The British and Irish team has two victories to its credit, both at St Andrews, and the last was in 1971, the fiftieth anniversary of the first informal match that was held in 1921.

ABOVE: *Jerry Pate, the US Amateur champion in 1974, successfully switched to the pro ranks.*

LEFT: *Hal Sutton was another US Amateur champion who made a smooth switch to the professionals.*

LEFT: *Jay Sigel – a true gentleman of the links and a leading amateur player.*

FAR LEFT: *Michael Bonallack holds the prestigious position of Secretary of the Royal and Ancient.*

BELOW LEFT: *Michael Bonallack during his playing days when he was five-times American Amateur champion.*

FACING PAGE: *Lanny Wadkins competing in the Open Championship at Troon in 1973, soon after turning professional.*

Britain will struggle to uncover once again a player of such prodigious talent as Michael Bonallack, a five-times winner of the Amateur Championship, and similarly the United States will find it difficult to replace Jay Sigel, a true gentleman of the links. In 1982 at the Country Club, Sigel, at the age of 38, and on his 16th attempt, won the US Amateur title when he beat David Tolley 8 and 7. He defended the title twelve months later when, at the North Shore Country Club, Glenview, Illinois, he beat Chris Perry 8 and 7 in the final to become the first back-to-back winner since Harvie Ward in 1955-56.

Sigel is the epitome of the amateur golfer, as was Bonallack who later became the secretary of the Royal and Ancient. When Sigel won the US Mid-Amateur in late 1987 there were those observers who suggested he might be the best amateur since Bobby Jones. That would unquestionably spark an intense discussion although Sigel most certainly deserved in 1984 to be the recipient of the Bobby Jones award which is presented annually by the United States Golf Association.

The award has landed in some noble golfing hands, notably Bonallack in 1972, Jack Nicklaus in 1975, JoAnne Carner in 1981, Tom Watson in 1987 and Arnold Palmer in 1971. The award is given to a person who has demonstrated outstanding personal qualities such as fair play, self-control and, perhaps, self-denial; generosity of spirit toward the game as a whole; and a manner of playing or behaving that shows respect for the game and the people in it.

If any one golfer can be singled out for possessing these qualities then it must be Arnold Daniel Palmer.

The Big Three

Arnold Palmer broke the ice when he won the US Masters in 1958. Then along came Gary Player and Jack Nicklaus. These three players, together referred to as the 'Big Three,' would dominate the golf scene in vastly contrasting manner, although there is no doubt whatsoever that Palmer was responsible for changing the game's image.

Palmer had grown up on a golf course. His father, MJ (Deke) Palmer was employed by a steel and electric company in Latrobe, Pennsylvania and he

became manager of a nine-hole course built there in 1921 some eight years before Arnold was born. Deke made extra money teaching during the Depression years and Arnold was born at a time when golf professionals were not expected to set foot in clubhouses.

The story goes that Arnold started his multi-million-pound empire at the age of nine. He had already learned the fundamentals of the game by spending much of his time with his father. He began using that experience to help women members at the club who struggled to hit their shots across the stream that cut the fourth fairway. He took their shots – for a few cents, of course!

Palmer, then, had the ability from a tender age not only to play the game but to sell his talent, and this unique combination of golfing skills and business acumen would pay handsome dividends throughout his career. Golfaholic Palmer benefited enormously from being guided by Mark McCormack the workaholic, but McCormack is the first to point out the reasons behind Palmer's astonishing business success. In his book *The Wonderful World of Professional Golf* McCormack writes about Palmer:

If you watch Palmer long enough with corporate executives you begin to appreciate why he gets along so well with them. Right or wrong, like it or not, a lot of high-level American business is conducted on the fairways and in the grill rooms of the country clubs.

The atmosphere is at once congenial, exclusive and fraternal. There is a universal challenge: the game. It puts everyone on common ground, and humbles all. The man it humbles least is a welcome and worthy inspiration in such circles. I wonder what value can be put on the phrase: 'As Arnold Palmer explained to me just the other day . . .' That is the currency of VIP golf. Palmer understands this. He maintains his role as star. Yet as he sits there in his cashmere with a company president and the chairman of a board, he knows he has his private jet waiting for him, just as they do. He is very much part of their world, and almost regally aware of it.

RIGHT: *A huge gallery follows the action at the Centenary Open Championship held at St Andrews in 1960.*

BELOW: *Kel Nagle, seen here playing at Moor Park in England, won the Centenary Open at St Andrews in 1960.*

Others, too, were to become aware of the importance of the business development of the game. Initially, however, Palmer had to prove himself on the fairways. He did so from 1958 to 1964 during which time he won the US Masters four times, the Open Championship twice and the US Open once.

Palmer, however, did much more than simply win championships. In 1960 it was his little piece of ideology that revitalized the Open Championship and gave birth to the return of the expression 'Grand Slam' for the first time since the great days of Bobby Jones. Palmer had won both the US Masters and the US Open in 1960 and he announced before setting out for the centenary Open Championship at St Andrews that he was making a bid to win both that Championship and the US PGA Championship. He claimed this was the modern day Grand Slam.

Palmer's idea won through, but he lost. He did not win the Open Championship that year, losing to the Australian Kel Nagle, and he never did win the US PGA Championship. It looked as if he might in 1960 after starting out with a 67, but in the end Jay Hebert emerged as the winner at the Firestone Country Club in Akron, Ohio.

Even so he became immensely popular on the fairways on both sides of the Atlantic. With his cavalier outlook he captured the public's imagination. He was the archetypal hero because even long-handicapped golfers could relate to his power-packed play.

LEFT: *Deane Beman, who became the Commissioner for the US PGA Tour.*

BELOW LEFT: *The scene at the clubhouse at Royal Birkdale, Lancashire, in 1961, after Arnold Palmer (holding the trophy aloft) had won the Open Championship.*

BELOW: *The money began to roll in, and Arnold Palmer is seen here driving during a special TV match held in 1961 against Gary Player at St Andrews – there was $10,000 at stake.*

RIGHT: *The legendary figure of Arnold Palmer studies the ball with intense concentration.*

FAR RIGHT: *The 16th hole at Cypress Point, California, where golf is played to the sound of the Pacific breaking on the rocks below.*

BELOW: *Arnold Palmer and his wife Winnie at a dinner held during the Bay Hill Classic in March 1979.*

The Palmer view was to go for broke – as he showed when he followed his first Open appearance in 1960 by returning to compete at Royal Birkdale in 1961. This time Palmer won, demonstrating his swash-buckling style with a stroke of such strength and skill that a plaque was placed to mark the spot.

Such accolades are not awarded lightly. The legendary Bobby Jones was given one at Royal Lytham and St Annes in 1926 after producing a shot at the 17th hole in the final round that is a part of the game's folklore. He was bunkered and his compatriot and rival for the title, Al Watrous, had negotiated the hole in two sound blows so that his ball was already safely on the putting surface. Jones stepped into the sand, facing a shot of some 170 yards, and with his mashie – a five iron – he clipped the ball over the scrubland and onto the green. Watrous, shell-shocked by this supreme stroke, three putted and Jones won the title. A plaque was later erected close to the point at which Jones executed his memorable

ABOVE: *Arnold Palmer earned plenty of money on the fairways. One of his most highly paid matches was with Bob Hope in the film* Call Me Bwana. *Bob Hope's club is probably the oddest Palmer has ever seen.*

ABOVE RIGHT: *Jack Nicklaus launched his professional career by winning the US Open at Oakmont when he beat Arnold Palmer in a play-off with a 71 to a 74. Here Jack grins as Arnold playfully punches him.*

RIGHT: *Members of the American Ryder Cup team of 1961 outside the Royal Lytham and St Annes clubhouse. They are (left to right) Jerry Barber, Jay Hebert, Arnold Palmer, Bill Collins, Dow Finsterwald, Art Wall Jnr, Bill Casper Jnr, Gene Littler, Mike Souchak and Doug Ford.*

shot. It simply says 'R T JONES JNR – The Open Championship – 25th June, 1926.'

Palmer gained similar immortality farther along the Lancashire coast with a great recovery also in the last round. It came at the 15th hole (which is now the 16th), where the powerful American had leaked his drive slightly too far to the right. The ball buried itself in heavy rough. Most golfers would have satisfied themselves with a recovery from there with a wedge. Palmer took a six iron from his bag and, with a tremendous swish, he hammered the ball some 140 yards so that it came to rest 15 feet from the hole. It was a high risk shot because he could have left the ball buried deeper in the rough.

Speaking later Palmer said, 'The rough was very deep. My only thought was to get the club through as hard as I could and maybe the ball would run onto the green. I closed the face slightly to get it through as fast as possible and I was amazed that I was able to get it through as fast as I did.'

LEFT: *Arnold Palmer in a reflective mood.*

BELOW: *Crowds at Wentworth came in their thousands to watch Arnold Palmer play in the 1971 Piccadilly World Match-Play Championship.*

RIGHT: *20-year-old Gary Player of South Africa won the Dunlop Tournament at Sunningdale in 1956. Here he receives £500 from Mr G E Beharrell.*

BELOW RIGHT: *Gary Player proudly displays the Open Championship trophy which he won for a third time, in 1974.*

PREVIOUS PAGES: *It was at Cherry Hills, Colorado, that the Arnold Palmer image was created in 1960. He was seven strokes behind with one round remaining when he daringly declared that 65 would be enough to win. He produced exactly that score to move past one rival after another and take the US Open for his first and only time.*

That, then, was the Palmer who captivated the British public, triggering an explosion of interest in the Open Championship, and he won again at Royal Troon in 1962. Palmer had not been present in 1959 at the Open Championship; there another golfer, later to become a cult figure in his own right, took the title at Muirfield. He was Gary Player and that first major victory for the little South African did not come easily. In fact he would shed tears before being crowned the champion.

In a typical rally that would become a trademark of his game, Player came from eight shots behind on the closing day – when 36 holes were played – to win. Yet he took six at the last and as he left the green so Player buried his head in his hands in the belief that he had thrown away his chance. His wife Vivienne stood by his side, whispering words of comfort, and it must have seemed an age before Player could smile once more. He had won by two strokes from Fred Bullock and Belgium's Flory van Donck.

Like the Australian Peter Thomson whom he had succeeded as Open champion, Gary Player was an extremely dedicated man. He had turned professional at the age of 18, intent on following in the footsteps of his illustrious compatriot Bobby Locke, and he did so with a few words of encouragement from Bobby Jones. When Player won the South African Open in 1956 his father wrote to Jones eulogizing the golfing talent of his son. Mr Player, however, was compelled to report that he could not afford to pay for his son to go to the United States but that if an invitation to the US Masters was received then he would pass the hat among his friends to see if they could obtain the necessary funds. The reply from Jones in August to Player in Johannesburg read simply 'Pass the Hat.'

This, then, was how Player made his debut in the 1956 US Masters, but it was at Augusta in 1961 that he was to have his first head-to-head duel with Palmer. Player won, with the assistance of a par at the last where he salvaged his four from a bunker,

although the tournament is probably best remembered as the one in which Palmer snatched defeat from the jaws of victory. For he came to the 18th hole needing only a par to beat Player. Instead he took six and he didn't even make it into a play-off. Palmer was in a greenside trap in two. He skulled the ball over the green, pitched back to eight feet and two putted. 'That is something I thought only happened to other people,' groaned Palmer.

LEFT: *Gary Player celebrates with his family following a record fifth win in the World Match-Play Championship at Wentworth, in 1973.*

BELOW: *Gary Player kisses the Open Championship trophy following his victory at Muirfield in 1959. He was then 23 years old and the youngest golfer to win the title since Scotland's fabled 'Young Tom' Morris in 1868.*

Player, however, had won the first of his three US Masters. He was also to win the US Open once – in 1965 – and the US PGA Championship twice, and he would also collect the Open Championship again in 1968 at Carnoustie and in 1974 at Royal Lytham and St Annes. This is a truly remarkable record of a very remarkable man. Because of his attire – he often dressed in an all-black outfit – Player was referred to as the 'Man in Black.' But that is less than skin deep. Gary Player is Mr Determination, a golfer with great commitment and a very positive thinker. When first starting out he never seemed a sure bet, and there is little about him that is orthodox. A fitness freak and food fanatic – he could be caught doing press-ups or eating dried fruit – he obtained the right rewards even if at times he was controversial and outspoken. He has won more than 140 tournaments around the world and when one considers the daunting thousands of miles he has been forced to travel from his South African home to many different venues worldwide his achievements probably match those of any other individual in the history of the game.

ABOVE: *Gary Player sprays sand into the air as he moves toward his third success in the US Masters with a last round of 64 in 1978.*

ABOVE LEFT: *Gary Player in action again in the 1976 World Match-Play Championship at Wentworth.*

LEFT: *The US PGA Championship trophy.*

FACING PAGE: *With his dedication and determination Gary Player has done much to promote the game of golf.*

ABOVE: *Jack Nicklaus practices as an amateur at Pebble Beach in 1961.*

ABOVE RIGHT: *Jack Nicklaus proudly holds the US Amateur trophy which he won in 1959.*

RIGHT: *Jack Nicklaus plays from the bunker at the 12th hole during the Open Championship at Troon in 1962.*

Yet when Player, the first overseas golfer to win the US Masters, challenged Palmer, so emerged the one man whose record would, rightly, go down in the history books as the greatest of any golfer. For if ever a word were coined in the English language to describe a giant of legendary stature it would fit Jack William Nicklaus to a tee in his role as a golfer.

So much has been said and written of Nicklaus and his awesome ability as a competitor that further words seem superfluous. He is without doubt regarded by most followers of the game as the greatest golfer ever. A statement as emphatic as this is not intended in any way to decry the achievements of such master golfers as Jones or Hagen, Palmer or Player. It is just that every now and then someone of the very highest caliber becomes a yardstick for measuring the achievements of others. In boxing it might be Muhammad Ali, in middle distance running Seb Coe, in tennis Bjorn Borg. If everyone were to vote for the best golfer ever then the likes of Jones, Hogan, Palmer, Sarazen, Player, Tom Watson and, let us not forget, Vardon would probably all have their supporters for one reason or another. Yet still Nicklaus would come out on top. He has to be seen as the number one golfer of all time.

Almost without doubt he could have equaled Bobby Jones's Grand Slam had he elected to remain an amateur. If evidence is needed then one has only to recall the events which unfolded in the US Open at Cherry Hills, Denver, Colorado in 1960. Mike Souchak led after three rounds on 208, but this most distinguished of fields included Nicklaus, still an amateur, and Ben Hogan, both on 211, Player on 213, Sam Snead on 214 and Palmer on 215. Nicklaus holed from 20 feet at the short 12th for a birdie two and at that point, with six holes remaining, he led. But as Hogan's hopes sank in the water at the 17th so Palmer continued a charge that would take him past Nicklaus. In fact he overtook no fewer than 14 players that famous last day, coming from seven shots off the

LEFT: *Jack Nicklaus in the rough at the Open Championship at St Andrews in 1964.*

BELOW LEFT: *Gary Player (right) wins the World Match-Play Championship once again in 1966 by beating Jack Nicklaus (left) 6 and 4 in the final at Wentworth.*

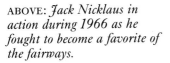
ABOVE: *Jack Nicklaus in action during 1966 as he fought to become a favorite of the fairways.*

pace. It has been correctly stated that a huge slice of the Palmer legend was born that day but also the American public realized that in Nicklaus they possessed another great golfer.

Not that they took to Nicklaus easily. Indeed he virtually became public enemy number one two years later at Oakmont Country Club in Palmer's state of Pennsylvania. His crime was to take on, and beat, Palmer in front of a record crowd of 62,000, many of whom formed the swarm of spectators who became known as 'Arnie's Army.' Nicklaus had won the US Amateur title the previous September and had then decided it was time to turn professional. At Oakmont, however, the pro-Palmer gallery regarded Nicklaus as an intruder. Palmer, raised only 40 miles away, was supposed to win and complete a triumphant return to the Pennsylvania heartland.

Arnie's Army, enlarged this time by a full brigade of iron and steel workers from Pittsburgh, did their level best to destroy Nicklaus. Yet he fought his way into a play-off with Palmer. It was a supreme achievement as Nicklaus, then a rather overweight, crew-cut athlete, had to endure jibe after jibe. 'Hey fatty,' shouted some members of the gallery. 'Hit the ball in here.' Those spectators were standing in the rough. Others yelled 'Hey, Crisco fat in the can.' (Crisco was a packaged cooking product.) And from another section of the crowd came the serious demands of 'Step on his ball, Arnie. Kick the thing into the rough.'

This, of course, was not what Palmer wanted. As the play-off unfolded so he genuinely pleaded with the fans to behave. The helmeted stewards struggled to keep order. Tempers rose beyond boiling point as Nicklaus began to take the initiative. Some reports

suggest that beer cans were thrown and that some reporters, there to cover this great head-to-head duel, were pushed into sand bunkers. Nicklaus, however, did not seem to notice the commotion. His blinkered approach took him to a 71 and Palmer, clearly distracted, shot 74. Jack Nicklaus had arrived and the world of golf now had the Big Three of Palmer, Player and Nicklaus.

Born in Columbus, Ohio in 1940 Nicklaus was playing golf at the age of ten. He was encouraged by his father Charles, and coached by Jack Grout. At the age of 12 he was breaking 80 and at 16 he was the Ohio State champion. In 1959 came his first US Amateur win after a keen tussle with Charles Coe.

So his career had followed a fairly comfortable path. Now the so-called 'fat boy' from the Keystone State would have to win the spectators on to his side.

Not that it seemed to bother him as he showed at Oakmont. He clearly understood the love that existed for Palmer and he knew there was one sure way to win the hearts of the supporters. He had to become the best golfer in the world.

Nicklaus had chosen a good time. Palmer's deeds had excited millions and encouraged a boom in the game. To understand the part that Nicklaus initially played it is important to realize that in America the emotions of the spectators move in highly mysterious but predictable ways. It is good to have a villain playing opposite the hero and in Nicklaus the American public had a perfectly cast villain. What right did this pudgy upstart from Columbus have to beat their flesh and blood superstar?

The evidence of the changes afoot in world golf can be illustrated by the fact that in 1963, for the first

ABOVE: *Muirfield, home of the Honourable Company of Edinburgh Golfers, is generally recognized as the oldest club in the world.*

RIGHT: *Bob Charles, the New Zealand left-hander, playing from the rough at the ninth hole during the Esso Golden Tournament at Moor Park, England, in July 1967.*

FAR RIGHT: *Gay Brewer after a long putt which just passes the hole during the World Match-Play Championship in 1967.*

BELOW: *Tony Lema fires his way out of the rough during the Open Championship at St Andrews in 1964 which he went on to win.*

time in the history of the US Tour, the leading money winner achieved six figures. The man at the top was Palmer with earnings of $128,230. Golf was becoming an attractive alternative for college kids who more and more took to the fairways rather than to football or baseball fields. So strong was the competition among would-be golfers that the US PGA elected in 1965 to launch a qualifying school for the Tour.

Around the world knowledge of the game was spreading, with countries such as Greece and Israel laying out their first courses in the early 1960s. But nowhere was the growth of the game accelerating as rapidly as it was in the United States. There the game grew at such a rate that by 1968 the tournament players had separated from the PGA to form their own body. Joe Dey was the first Commissioner and prize money began to rocket. The US Tour had been worth $150,000 in 1938. By 1952 the figure was $500,000 then by 1973 $8 million and today it approaches $30 million.

Palmer continued to play a leading role in the promotion of the game. Even so he ceased to be a force in the major championships. Player would have his moments such as at the US Masters in 1978 when he won the title for a third time with an astonishing Palmer-type last round charge in which he birdied seven of the last ten holes. He did so alongside one Severiano Ballesteros, of whom much more would be heard, and he went on to complete a quite unique hat-trick by winning the Tournament of Champions, then the Houston Open.

This, however, was the era of Nicklaus. Two years after turning professional Nicklaus was, in 1963, the second player to earn more than $100,000 in one season. The figure grew with his victories to more than $200,000 in 1971, more than $300,000 in 1973 and, as others took over the individual seasonal records, so Nicklaus was overall the leading money winner. Although in July 1968 Palmer became the first player to earn more than $1 million in official winnings on the US Tour, Nicklaus was the first to make it to $2 million (December 1973), $3 million (May 1977), $4 million (February 1983) and then $5 million in 1987.

His first US Masters win came in 1963 when, although five shots behind he came through to get his first fitting of the famous green jacket which was awarded annually to the custodian of the championship. He followed that performance later in the year by winning the US PGA Championship for the first time when he came home ahead of Dave Regan Junior at the Dallas Athletic Club in Texas. The old green jacket was his again in 1965 at Augusta National where he was in magnificent form. His first round of 67 put him two strokes behind Player. In the second round he drew level with Player and Palmer. Then it happened – he burst out of the field with a record 64 which included eight birdies, ten pars and not a five in his card. His devastating drives, around the 300 yard mark, were power strokes of some magnitude. Nicklaus set a new record aggregate of 271 and he won by a record margin of nine strokes.

LEFT: *Roberto de Vicenzo of Argentina sits downcast (left) following the US Masters in 1968. He had signed an incorrect card and so gave victory to Bob Goalby of the United States.*

ABOVE: *Jack Nicklaus demonstrates his mastery as he drives from a sand trap.*

It was not until his fifth assault on the Open Championship, at Muirfield in 1966, that he finally won. By then the prize money had increased by 20 percent from the previous year when the Australian Peter Thomson had regained the silver claret jug following victories by New Zealand's Bob Charles and America's Tony Lema in 1963 and 1964.

Thomson's win in 1965 had been much deserved. Some had commented that by not taking on the best in the United States Thomson had himself highlighted a flaw in his universal ability. And that when he was winning Open Championships in the 1950s there were not many Americans in the field at the time to challenge him. It was also cruelly said of him that he had no taste for courses in the United States which were not suited to his style. That the larger American ball had less appeal to Thomson is almost certainly nearer the truth.

But Thomson needs no defense of his ability. It was there for all to see including the American public as he won the Texas Open in 1956. He was a highly skilled craftsman who compensated for his lack of length by scrambling with a highly adept touch. He played an active role in public life, his concern for others evident in his work for an antidrugs organization. In 1965 he answered his critics with a marvelous performance.

In 1966, however, the British public had a new champion. It was Nicklaus's turn and he won from his compatriot Doug Sanders and the Welshman David Thomas. Nicklaus was a true master from tee to green. His campaign for perfection often meant that he stood most of the day on the practice range. He would blister his hands hitting around 500 balls and consoled himself with the knowledge that it was turning him into the world's finest golfer.

ABOVE: *Jack Nicklaus can sense that he is on the way to a famous comeback triumph at Augusta in 1986.*

ABOVE LEFT: *Jack Nicklaus lines up a putt at the US Masters in 1986, while his son Jack Junior, who was caddie, looks over his shoulder.*

LEFT: *A broad grin sweeps across Jack Nicklaus's face as Bernhard Langer helps him into the traditional green jacket after his fine victory in 1986.*

RIGHT: *Jack Nicklaus is seen here driving at the 18th hole at Augusta with the Australian Greg Norman also on the tee.*

Nicklaus's first Open Championship came in the same year that it was decided to play the event over four days instead of packing the final two rounds into one day. Thus it was stretched through to the Saturday and the era of the true tournament professional had arrived. In the past it had been felt that most professionals would have to be back at their club posts for the weekend to cater to the members. Life too was changing on the British fairways as far as the professionals were concerned although the massive increases in prize money would in reality not reach Europe until the 1980s.

Even so the Open Championship was now flourishing. Palmer had done his work and whereas before his arrival television coverage had consisted of barely one hour's play, by 1967 the ABC TV company had purchased American rights as a forerunner to the Championship being screened to millions of viewers all over the world. The victory of the popular Argentinian Roberto de Vicenzo was one to cherish in 1967 as he came home at Hoylake, although there was to be disappointment for him the following year when he lost the US Masters by signing for a wrong score. Officials searched for a way out for Vicenzo, whose only crime had been to sign the card without checking it, but they were nevertheless compelled to abide by the rules of the game.

Nicklaus, of course, continued with his winning ways. Even so, players like Gay Brewer, Bob Goalby, who benefited at Vicenzo's expense, and George Archer took the US Masters title in 1967, 1968 and 1969 respectively. It was the US Open of 1968, however, that unearthed the first real challenger to

Nicklaus's reign on the golfing throne. His name was Lee Buck Trevino and with his rounds of 69, 68, 69 and 69 at Oak Hill, Rochester, New York, he became the first player in the history of the US Open to play four sub-70 rounds.

What is more he matched Nicklaus's one-year-old record aggregate for the US Open of 275 and he pushed Nicklaus into the runner's-up berth. The Trevino story reads like a boys' adventure story. He came from the other side of the tracks in Dallas, Texas and he worked his way up to become the Four Million Dollar Man on the US Tour.

The kid was first introduced to golf around the age of seven when he helped out on a local golf range. The man who ran the place, Hardy Greenwood, set Lee on the way with a little push, a lot of guidance and his first set of clubs. Lee stayed on at the range until he joined the US Marine Corps. He served for about four years and then became the assistant in the professional shop at El Paso, Texas. This experience was to stand him in good stead later in life when on the road to golfing fame. He picked up the golf lingo and chit-chat, and his pleasing personality made him a natural hit wherever he played.

ABOVE: *Lee Trevino (left), golf's joker of the pack, provides the fans with something to laugh about as he explains to British comedian Bruce Forsyth how he missed a putt in 1971 at Royal Birkdale.*

LEFT: *Liang Huan Lu, or 'Mr Lu' as he became known, of Formosa, came within one shot of creating a little slice of history. Lee Trevino won the Open Championship there but 'Mr Lu' finished runner-up only one shot back.*

RIGHT: *With his laugh-a-minute antics, Lee Trevino is a popular figure on the golfing circuit.*

FAR RIGHT: *Lee Trevino keeps smiling even though his title is slipping away at the US PGA Championship at Cherry Hills in 1985. Hubert Green was the winner.*

BELOW: *The charismatic Lee Trevino dances during the US Open at Shinnecock Hills in 1986 in which Raymond Floyd triumphed.*

In 1965 he won the Texas State Open and he began moving up. He finished fifth behind Nicklaus in the 1967 US Open at Baltusrol, Springfield, New Jersey and by this stage was playing the full tournament circuit. But it was at the US Open the following year that he really made his mark. His opening two rounds put him five in the lead over Nicklaus. He was caught, however, and overtaken by Bert Yancey. What a contrasting sight they made. There was the laugh-a-minute Trevino, the stocky former gun sergeant, and Yancey, who had been a cadet at West Point and who was recognized for his classic swing. Not so for Trevino who went to work with an unorthodox open stance.

Trevino, however, started to chip away at Yancey's lead. It was not classic stuff in the last round but Trevino's putting was canceling any errors he made on the way to the green. Nicklaus had lost ground and with Yancey faltering so Lee Trevino was able to take the title.

It was at around this time on the other side of the Atlantic that another challenger emerged for Nicklaus. His name was Tony Jacklin. He was the son of a locomotive driver from Scunthorpe in England. His arrival would launch the golf boom in Britain and subsequently on the European continent. Jacklin was to enjoy a highly profitable career; his most cherished moments came at Royal Lytham and St Annes in 1969 when he won the Open Championship, and at Hazeltine, Chaska, Minneapolis 11 months later when he won the US Open.

ABOVE: *Lee Trevino (right) simply can't stop clowning and here he is during a TV match at Turnberry watched by professional 'opponent' Seve Ballesteros (extreme left) and interviewed by Peter Alliss. Howard Keel, next to Lee, joins in the laughter.*

LEFT: *Tony Jacklin, who in 1969 became the first British winner of the Open Championship since Max Faulkner in 1951.*

RIGHT: *Tony Jacklin's exploits lit the blue touch paper on a golfing explosion in Europe.*

Inbetween those wins came an historic and touching moment for both Jacklin and Nicklaus. It occurred in the autumn of 1969 at Royal Birkdale where Great Britain and Ireland were locked in battle with the United States for the Ryder Cup. The inaugural Ryder Cup contest had been held in 1927 although there had been a match at Gleneagles six years earlier when the Americans lost, and another informal affair in 1926. After four official matches the overall score stood at 2-2. By the time the 1969 match unfolded it was 14-3 in the United States' favor!

Jacklin and Nicklaus would have other scraps, as opposing captains in the Ryder Cup but their duel as players at Royal Birkdale will live long in the memory of all those who witnessed it. On the last green Nicklaus moved quickly over to Jacklin's ball marker, which was some three feet from the hole, and he picked it up. With that generous gesture he ensured that for the first time in the history of the match the result would be a tie.

What is more, it was the kind of sporting act which would win Nicklaus support in Britain. He had won his first battle, against the army of fans who cheered Palmer and jeered him, and he now wanted to endorse that feeling across the Atlantic. He went much of the way that afternoon on the Lancashire coast, but it was surely at St Andrews in 1970 that he won the day.

Nicklaus had not won a major championship since the US Open in 1967. Billy Casper had beaten Gene Littler in a play-off for the US Masters earlier in 1970 after which Jacklin had become the first British winner of the US Open since Ted Ray in 1920. With such results, plus the emergence of

RIGHT: *Tony Jacklin with his wife Viv and their children (left to right) Warren, Bradley and Tina.*

Trevino, there was a threat to Nicklaus. Like all great stars he was being placed under increasing pressure through his absence from the winners' circle of the championships that really matter.

In effect he was helped at St Andrews in that summer of 1970 when Doug Sanders took three putts – missing from three feet – on the last green. This produced a tie and Nicklaus won the play-off by playing the last hole in great style. He peeled off his sweater, hit an almighty drive, and the ball actually went over the green. But he chipped back down to six feet, then holed for a birdie that kept him ahead of Sanders with a 72 to a 73.

Jacklin had covered the opening nine holes in the first round that year at St Andrews in 29 strokes. It was an amazing start to a title defense, but he was sabotaged by a thunderstorm. Play was stopped and when Jacklin returned the following day the magic had left his game. He might have won again in 1971, but Trevino triumphed. In 1972 at Muirfield Trevino ended Jacklin's brief challenge to Nicklaus for world supremacy by twice holing out in the third round, then providing the ultimate in killing blows at the 17th on the final day. Lee said later, 'God is a Mexican!'

It seemed that Jacklin, on the green in three at the par five and only 15 feet from the hole, was ready to win again. Then Trevino, who had virtually given up all hope of winning, contrived to chip in from off the green for the unlikeliest of par fives while Jacklin three putted for a six.

Killer shots such as these can deliver such a psychological blow to a player that they can unnerve him completely. That happened to Jacklin who would no longer be the force that he had once been.

LEFT: Peter Alliss commentating for BBC television.

BELOW LEFT: Members of the victorious American Ryder Cup team celebrate with the trophy at Muirfield in 1973. Jackie Burke, the captain, receives a helping hand from (left to right) Lee Trevino, Dave Hill, Billy Casper and J C Snead.

BELOW: Billy Casper pictured in 1966 when he won the US Open Championship at the Olympic Club, San Francisco.

Trevino, however, was doing his level best to push Nicklaus to one side. He had a marvelous set-to with Nicklaus in the US Open at Merion in 1971 where they finished level. Trevino won the play-off with a 68 to a 71 and, laughing and joking throughout, he named Nicklaus the world's best golfer.

After his success at Muirfield Trevino won two US Opens and two British Opens as well as the first of his two US PGA Championships – the other came during a revival in 1984 – at Tanglewood, Winston-Salem, North Carolina in 1974.

At the Western Open in 1975, however, Trevino was struck by lightning – he was thankful that his life was spared – and from that moment he was bugged with back trouble. Trevino was not a quitter and he soldiered on despite a rapid decline. Then in 1984 'Super Mex,' as he is fondly known, came back to win the US PGA Championship again at Shoal Creek, Birmingham, Alabama, with Player and Lanny Wadkins sharing the runner's-up spot.

It was no less than he deserved. Lee Trevino had added a smile to the face of competitive golf. His sense of humor, like donning a top hat and tails in Britain at the start of the Alcan Golfer of the Year Tournament at a time when there was talk about his dress sense, was like a breath of fresh air. He had a marvelous rapport with the galleries of spectators which few, if any, have ever equaled. It is said that it is best to laugh at life. Lee continues to laugh at golf – at what it did for him and what he did for it.

Nicklaus, however, remained the King as the seventies unfolded. He had dethroned Palmer, kept Player at arm's length and parried the thrusts of Jacklin and Trevino. Yet there were bigger battles to be fought by the man who was now loved by the spectators everywhere. The 'Golden Bear,' as he was now known, would have to huff and puff and blow a few more challengers away.

FAR LEFT ABOVE: *Members of the Royal and Ancient Golf Club watch from the 'Big Room' of the clubhouse as the final stages of the 1967 Alcan Golfer of the Year Championship unfold at St Andrews. Gay Brewer of the United States won the title.*

FAR LEFT BELOW: *Jack Nicklaus (left), then the defending champion, and Arnold Palmer share a joke. During the late sixties and seventies Nicklaus dethroned Palmer to become the king of the fairways.*

LEFT: *Jack Nicklaus (second from left) sets out for the start of another day in the 1986 US Open at Shinnecock Hills.*

The Power Struggle

FAR RIGHT: *Johnny Miller won the US Open in 1973 and the British equivalent three years later.*

BELOW RIGHT: *Tom Weiskopf lines up a putt on the ninth green at Walton Heath, England, during the 1978 European Open which was won by his compatriot Bobby Wadkins. The superstitious Weiskopf had vowed not to shave off his beard until the end of the tournament.*

The seventies would see a dazzling display of stirring performances from Jack Nicklaus. He won in 1971, apart from the US PGA Championship, four other events on the American circuit including the national team title with Arnold Palmer. In 1972 he took seven titles, including the US Masters and the US Open, and there were to be seven victories again in 1973. These included the US PGA Championship – one month after he had finished fourth in the Open Championship at Royal Troon behind Tom Weiskopf and Johnny Miller.

The persistence of Nicklaus would face two new rivals in Miller who had won the US Open earlier in 1973 at Oakmont, and Weiskopf. At Troon Weiskopf

LEFT: *Johnny Miller, the golden boy from California, playing his second shot to the 17th green at Muirfield during the 1972 Open Championship. In 1974 he won five of the first 11 events on the US Tour – an astounding achievement. During that time his golf was of a standard that very few players in the history of the game have attained.*

had overcome the wet conditions to register an important win whereas Miller, newer to the scene, was about to set the US Tour alight with no fewer than eight wins in 1974 – including the first three of the season – as he rocketed to number one in the official money list. He had first gained national notoriety when, after signing up to caddie at the 1966 US Open at the Olympic Club in his home town of San Francisco, he actually qualified to compete. He eventually finished joint eighth. It was not until the 1973 US Open, however, that he earned global respect when he achieved a sparkling last round of 63.

ABOVE: *Tom Weiskopf kisses the trophy as he basks in the glory of being the 1973 Open champion following a fine performance at Royal Troon.*

RIGHT: *Weiskopf swings into a new year on 1 January 1982, but it would not be long before he moved into semiretirement.*

FAR RIGHT: *Johnny Miller during the US Open at Shinnecock Hills in 1986. Miller had one of the best putting touches in the business during the 1970s.*

Miller, the golden boy from California, had claimed stardom with a powerful and precise game coupled with a wonderful touch on the greens. He had, in one sense, emerged from nowhere. In contrast Weiskopf's success at Troon only cemented the belief that here was the man with the finest swing in golf at the time, a swing both smooth and predictable. Perhaps because he was born in Ohio Weiskopf was seen as a rival to Nicklaus who also came from that state. In fact it was a comparison which did Weiskopf little good for at times he came under a great deal of pressure because of the association.

Even so with Nicklaus not winning a major championship in 1974 – Gary Player took the US Masters and the Open Championship, Hale Irwin the US Open at Winged Foot, Mamaroneck, New York and Lee Trevino the US PGA Championship at Tanglewood, North Carolina – Miller and Weiskopf were regarded as the new breed. Nicklaus, however, emphasized at Augusta in the spring of 1975 that he was ready to meet their challenge. The 'Golden Bear,' now much loved by the American public, flourished amid the azaleas and the dogwood to score an emphatic victory in the US Masters.

It was a classic ding-dong encounter all the way. Nicklaus departed from his usual practice of launching last round charges to lead the way with opening rounds of 68 and 67. In the third round, however, he faltered by taking 73. Miller, 11 shots behind at the

halfway stage, could thus pick up eight of these with a 65. Meanwhile Weiskopf edged ahead of Nicklaus with a 66. The scene was set for a quite extraordinary final day during which any one of these three players might have won. Miller's outward 32, including five birdies, was the stuff of champions. Weiskopf, however, remained in front. He was paired with Miller, and Nicklaus was playing ahead.

Nicklaus, however, seemed to hold the upper hand as, with six holes remaining, he led by one from Weiskopf with Miller a further two shots adrift. Miller was the only one of the three to extract a birdie from the long 13th. Nicklaus dropped a shot at the 14th and Weiskopf, playing the hole some ten minutes later, made a birdie. Weiskopf was back in the lead but Nicklaus made a birdie at the long 15th, hitting a superb one iron into the heart of the green. It seemed likely to be a crucial blow when Weiskopf's approach skipped over the green but he chipped back to 15 feet from where he holed for a birdie. It kept him ahead at 12 under par, with Nicklaus in hot competition at 11 under and Miller, who had also birdied the 15th, now at 10 under.

There comes a time, however, in any sport when an individual becomes a true champion of the game. This was Nicklaus's moment. Weiskopf had every right to feel, as he walked onto the 16th tee, that he was at last going to win a championship by extinguishing Nicklaus's flame. He looked ahead and he could see that Nicklaus was some 40 feet from the hole. Nicklaus could three putt from there.

Then came the moment of reality for Weiskopf. Nicklaus hit his putt and the ball raced toward the cup. Then it disappeared and, as Nicklaus extended his putter high above his head in a gesture of delight, so Weiskopf was aware that the initiative had swung back into the hands of his rival. Weiskopf waited, hoping to instill the level-headed confidence he now required, but his shot came up some 35 yards short. He took three to get down.

ABOVE: *Hale Irwin won the Piccadilly World Match-Play Championship in successive years in 1974 and 1975 at Wentworth, England.*

RIGHT: *A view of the 16th green at Augusta as another US Masters reaches its climax.*

It wasn't over – although, perhaps, in retrospect it was. Miller, as he was inclined to do in such situations, made a birdie at the 17th so that both he and Weiskopf now required a birdie at the last to tie with Nicklaus. Weiskopf struck at that 18th hole that travels uphill toward the cloistered Augusta clubhouse, a prodigious drive. He had hit the ball about 50 yards past Miller and he needed only a nine iron for his approach. Miller, playing first, hit his shot to 20 feet; Weiskopf, as if under no pressure whatsoever, struck his to ten feet. Nicklaus, however, had done enough. He was in the clubhouse and the pressure was on his opponents to hole their putts. They failed. And Nicklaus became the Five Star Champion of the Masters Tournament. Weiskopf, for a fourth time, had finished in the runner's-up spot. The glory of Augusta would never be his and Nicklaus had seen to it that another of his challengers had been compelled to accept defeat.

To his eternal credit Miller would take on Nicklaus once more in the Open Championship at Royal Birkdale in 1976. This time he would win, with Nicklaus forced to accept a share of second place along with a precocious Spaniard called Severiano Balles-

teros. It would appear to the majority of observers that the era of Miller had begun.

That, however, was not to be. Instead Tom Watson, a young, freckle-faced kid from Kansas City who became known as the Huckleberry Finn of golf, offered Nicklaus a new challenge. He had revealed to British spectators that he possessed a solid game and an efficient, almost mechanical, putting method, by winning the Open Championship at Carnoustie in 1975. There he had beaten Jack Newton, the Australian, with a 71 to a 72 in a play-off. Watson endeared himself to the British public because he belonged to that enviable breed who get on with the game without any fuss. When a shot finished in a bunker, he even smiled, showing he was human.

Watson had started out, like so many other youngsters, by being introduced to the game by his father. Tom, born in Kansas City in September 1949, was six years old at the time and his father was a scratch golfer. The young Watson was quick to respond to tuition and he went on to become a four-times winner of the Missouri State Amateur and to play for three years at Stanford University, before graduating in 1971 with a degree in psychology.

ABOVE: *Jack Newton (left) of Australia, and Tom Watson of the United States, hold the Open Championship trophy after 72 holes of intense competition at Carnoustie in 1975. Watson, however, went on to win the play-off and the first of his five Opens. Sadly Newton's career came to an abrupt end after he lost his right arm in an aircraft accident.*

ABOVE LEFT: *Lou Graham claimed the US Open title at Medinah, Illinois, in 1975 following a play-off with John Mahaffey.*

RIGHT: *The road which leads to the clubhouse at Augusta and possibly fame and fortune in the US Masters.*

FAR RIGHT ABOVE: *Jack Newton plays from the semirough at the fifth hole at Carnoustie during his play-off with Tom Watson at the Open Championship in 1975.*

FAR RIGHT BELOW: *Hale Irwin driving during his match with Australia's David Graham in the World Match-Play Championship at Wentworth, England in 1983. Irwin won 2 and 1.*

ABOVE: *Tom Watson driving during his classic showdown for the Open Championship with Jack Nicklaus at Turnberry in 1977.*

RIGHT: *A trio of great American golfers, (left to right) Jack Nicklaus, Tom Watson and Tom Weiskopf, at Muirfield in 1980 when Tom Watson won the third of his five titles.*

Watson turned professional in 1972 and slowly but surely he began to make his mark on the game. The trouble for American observers, even after Watson's win in the Western Open on the brutal Butler National course in 1974, was in deciding whether or not he was a bona fide challenger. Yes, he had won at Carnoustie, but no, he had lost the US Opens of 1974 and 1975 – Hale Irwin and Lou Graham had won – after being in challenging positions. Some had cruelly chosen to call Watson a 'choker,' a reference to the fact that he was unable to stand up to the pressure.

The Open Championship, however, had at least provided a launch pad for Watson. He was convinced that if he could win at Carnoustie then he could win other major championships. What is more he also won the World Series of Golf in 1975 which, although only a four-man series then, included the cream of the game. Yet it was not until 1977 that it really began to happen for Watson. First he won the US Masters, earning a stream of complimentary remarks about his future, notably from Nicklaus, and then he went head to head with Nicklaus for the Open Championship at Turnberry in one of the most fascinating encounters in the history of golf.

Coincidentally when Nicklaus put down the challenges of Miller and Weiskopf in the 1975 US Masters, his playing partner on the final day was none other than Tom Sturges Watson. That taste of the power and the glory of the game had driven Watson, two months later, into a clear lead in the US Open at Medinah, where, however, he would finish with rounds of 78 and 77. Hence the 'choker' reputation.

If there was any truth in that reputation then surely at Augusta in 1977 Watson should have taken five at the 11th instead of chipping to two feet, saving his par, after watching Nicklaus who was ahead of him, close to within one shot with a 12-foot birdie putt at the short 12th. The challenge was on and Nicklaus seemed to suggest so when he tapped in for a birdie four at the long 13th. Watson was standing in the middle of the fairway at the time waiting to play his next shot and Nicklaus, leaving the green, raised his arm and looked back down the fairway. There were many at that moment, including Watson, who viewed that as a challenging gesture. Nicklaus insisted later that he would never do such a thing and Watson accepted Nicklaus's explanation and apologized for thinking he might.

Nevertheless it heightened the drama at the time. Watson felt his lips dry. He knew this was the moment, that the last hour on this great golf course could possibly decide his place in the game. If he could beat Nicklaus now then he would erase that 'choker' image. He wasn't worried by it but he could not ignore it. And what better place to prove his ability to the doubting Thomases than Augusta. Sadly Bobby Jones was not there to see this great drama unfold but if he had been then surely he would, like the rest of those who were present, have congratulated Watson. For as early as 1965 Jones had declared: 'Jack Nicklaus plays a game of which I am not familiar.' It was a reference to his admiration for Nicklaus and that admiration would have extended to any player who was capable of taking on and then beating the formidable Golden Bear.

LEFT: *Tom Watson practicing his driving on the range in 1984.*

LEFT: *Tom Watson reflects studiously. The top money winner in the United States for four years in succession, from 1977 to 1980, he was also the first golfer to earn more than $500,000 in one season.*

ABOVE: *A classic shot of a classic course: Turnberry came onto the Open Championship rota in 1977 and it was an immediate success. The Ailsa course is not only a supreme examination but it is one of the best courses on which to watch both the golf and the outstanding views looking west toward the Isle of Arran and the Mull of Kintyre.*

Watson, however, looked as if he might crumble when he took five at the 14th, so losing the outright lead. Moreover Nicklaus extracted a birdie four from the long 15th to go one ahead as revealed by the giant leader boards of Augusta. Watson, however, reached the 15th with a drive and a two iron and he putted for a birdie, as Nicklaus parred the 16th ahead of him. In fact it was not until Nicklaus stood in the middle of the 18th fairway that another huge roar ascended from the spectators as those standing near the 17th watched Watson's birdie from 20 feet topple into the cup. It was a deafening blow for Nicklaus. The great champion hit behind his ball with a six iron and the

ball finished short of the green in a bunker. The duel was over and Watson, the David of the piece, had slain the Goliath of golf.

The talk across the length and breadth of the United States was of Nicklaus and Watson meeting head to head again in the US Open at Southern Hills, Tulsa, Oklahoma. This was not to be, for there Hubert Green outlasted Lou Graham. Even so the golfing populace did not have to wait long. Nicklaus and Watson would, like two golfing gunfighters, duel again that summer at Turnberry for the Open Championship. The event was a classic.

The Royal and Ancient had chosen in 1977 to put

ABOVE: *The lighthouse at Turnberry is conveniently positioned to flash a warning to those in peril on the tee.*

LEFT: *Tom Watson looks anxious, although there was no need to as he steered his way toward Open Championship glory at Turnberry in 1977.*

Turnberry on the map. It would join the Open Championship rota along with St Andrews, Muirfield and Royal Troon in Scotland, and Royal Birkdale, Royal Lytham and St Annes and Royal St George's in England. Carnoustie was to fall by the wayside and for Turnberry it was quite a miracle that golf was being played there. Even before the evolution of golf the countryside had been scarred by the battles of yesteryear with kings like Robert the Bruce defending their castles. The events of the Second World War, when tarmac strips were laid across Turnberry's springy turf so spoiling the courses, were even more damaging to the countryside.

RIGHT: *The 1977 Championship at Turnberry with Tom Watson walking toward his ball along with his caddie, Alfie Fyles.*

Following the war, however, Scottish architect Mackenzie Ross helped repair the course at Turnberry and this now became the arena for what many people regard as the most exciting Open Championship in the history of the sport.

All eyes were trained from the start on Jack Nicklaus, the 'King,' and Tom Watson, the 'Crown Prince.' Yet few could have predicted, as they both opened with rounds of 68 and 70, what would eventually unfold. These two supreme golfers simply engaged in a fascinating duel. Nicklaus first in front, then Watson coming back, and for the excited spectators it was quite magical entertainment. Only a thunderstorm would interrupt them during a sweltering third day. Nicklaus and Watson sought refuge among the rocks, and this provided a brief interlude for the two golfers to ponder the situation or look out to sea to Ailsa Craig, a rocky islet in the Firth of Clyde, and to the peaks of Arran. Then it was back to business as the two golfers kept the tension running high when they completed 65s to remain locked in the lead.

The sun shone on Turnberry on that final day and on Nicklaus for the first four holes. By that time he had moved three strokes ahead and it seemed he was out for a stroll. Watson, however, had won his badge of courage three months earlier at Augusta. He could now digest such turnarounds and, more important, he could come back. He birdied the fifth, seventh and eighth, and as the spectators rushed from hole to hole, so the officials were compelled to call a short halt. When play resumed Watson bogeyed the ninth – he was one behind again. Nicklaus's 25-foot birdie putt at the 12th gave him a two-stroke lead.

Watson retaliated with a putt of 12 feet for a birdie at the 13th. He turned to Nicklaus, remarking 'Is this what it's all about, Jack?' Back came the answer, swift and succinct, 'Right, Tom.' Nicklaus, still one ahead, naturally knew that the unpredictable nature of the game meant that this Open Championship was far from over. However, he can be forgiven for feeling, even today, that he was robbed of the initiative by an audacious stroke at the 15th. There Watson rolled the ball in from 60 feet for a two. The shot gave Watson the momentum to go on and birdie the 17th, so that in three holes he had come from one behind to one ahead at the most crucial time in the match.

The game must have seemed a foregone conclusion at the 18th when Watson drilled a magnificent seven-iron approach to within 18 inches of the flag. Nicklaus's second had finished some 30 feet away from the cup. He would need to hole that to put pressure on Watson. The odds against doing so must have been heavily stacked against him, but in the ball went. The gallery could hardly believe it. Now Watson had to make his putt. It still measured only 18 inches in length but as Nicklaus accepted the applause of the congregation so Watson must have felt in his heart that the putt was growing longer all the time. But he made no mistake and the title was his.

It had been the classic to beat all classics. Watson had fired a last round of 65 to Nicklaus's 66 and he had won the second of his five Open Championships. If any one player truly challenged Nicklaus when he was at the height of his game, then it must be Watson. He set new standards and smashed records, emerging on no less than six occasions between 1977 and

LEFT: *Isao Aoki was for many years the number one golfer in Japan. He gave the world a new putting technique of holding the club so that the heel was placed firmly on the ground and the toe pointed skyward.*

BELOW: *Aoki lines up a putt before moving into action with his unique putting style.*

1984 as Player of the Year in the United States and five times the leading money winner. He was also to win the US Masters again in 1981 although he must have gained greater satisfaction with his US Open success at Pebble Beach in 1982. There, on the Californian coast, it was almost like Turnberry revisited.

This time Nicklaus and Watson were not paired together and it was Nicklaus who finished first. He shot a last round of 69 – an excellent performance on the Pebble Beach course which is regarded by many golfing experts as the eighth wonder of the world. This meant that Watson would need to make a birdie at one of the two remaining holes. That seemed most unlikely to Nicklaus as he signed his card. For the news was that Watson had missed the green at the short 17th. He faced the prospect of taking four, since his ball was buried in a collar of grass between two bunkers. There was only 30 feet between him and the hole but it seemed impossible for Watson to get the ball close. The ball would, however, come out of that ankle-deep rough fast and, with only 12 feet of green with which to work, this was one of those 10,000-1 make-or-break shots. Such was Watson's confidence that, as his caddie, hoping to inspire his employer, whispered, 'Get it close, Tom,' so he replied, 'I'll do better than that – I'll make it!'

Players of Watson's class immediately know when they have executed the perfect shot. As he bumped the ball forward so Watson yelled, 'It's going in – I know it's going in!' It did, and Nicklaus, deflated, observed, 'Tom could have gone back there and hit that shot one thousand times and he would not have made it.'

A dream for Nicklaus had been dashed. He had hoped at Pebble Beach to win a record fifth US Open which would push him ahead of Anderson, Hogan and Jones. Nicklaus would have to wait until 1986 for another major championship, although when it came, at Augusta, he would not only establish another record with a sixth US Masters title but would unquestionably prove that he could still put down those 'upstarts' who assumed they could relieve him of the number one tag.

Watson had made a gallant effort and with his Open Championship win at Royal Birkdale in 1983 he did move to within one more victory of equaling Harry Vardon's record of six successes. Nicklaus will never make that total – Watson might – but who will ever match Nicklaus's achievement in winning six US Masters, five US PGA Championships, four US Opens, three US Masters and two US Amateur Championships?

Even so times were changing. The gospel of golf had spread to such an extent that as Nicklaus and Watson dueled for supremacy so the scene was also enlivened by the arrival of newcomers such as Severiano Ballesteros of Spain, Bernhard Langer, of West Germany, Greg Norman of Australia, and the British golfers Nick Faldo and Sandy Lyle. The popularity of golf owes much to the intense coverage provided by television and other media. Knowledge of the game was initially limited to a chosen few and it should be remembered that the first official golf tour took place only in 1903 when the Oxford and Cambridge Golfing Society went to the United States.

What is more, while there might have been championships in places such as Australia and South Africa during the 1900s it was not until the 1930s that the game of golf made spectacular progress. The game that had been created by the Scots or the Dutch, depending on which historians you choose to believe, was most certainly popularized by the Americans. Many more golf courses were constructed in the United States, with the result that today nearly 20 million people play the game in that country alone.

As world travel became easier, so Americans extended their influence to other parts of the globe, with the result that players such as Palmer began to encourage the building of golf courses in places as far afield as China. There, with his architect Ed Seay, he laid out in 1982 the Chung Shan Hot Spring golf course. China was back on the golfing map for the first time since 1949 when golf had been decreed a bourgeois pastime and the few courses that existed had been turned into paddy fields.

The likes of Player and Locke, from South Africa, Nagle and Thomson, from Australia, Bob Charles from New Zealand and Roberto de Vicenzo from Argentina, gave golf an international flavor. Yet it was not until such golfers as Ballesteros and Langer, Lyle and Norman, that Americans faced a

truly serious threat to their supremacy in world golf.

Gary Player remains probably the finest example of a non-American to compete successfully around the world. David Graham of Australia, too has a fine record, with the 1979 US PGA Championship and the 1981 US Open to his credit. Greg Norman is a further example of a golfer from Down Under whose performance has been astonishing. In 1986 Norman won the Open Championship at Turnberry and later that year he finished at the top of the US Tour money list. To take on the cream of American golf week by week and to become the first 'overseas' winner of the official money list since Gary Player in 1961 is a very impressive and laudable achievement.

ABOVE: *Manuel Pinero, the son of a pig farmer, from Badajoz in Spain, near the Portuguese border, launched an outstanding career by winning the Madrid Open in 1974. His finest hour came when he won the PGA Championship in 1977.*

LEFT: *Seve Ballesteros celebrates on the 18th green following his Open Championship win at Royal Lytham and St Annes in 1979.*

ABOVE: *The umbrellas come out at Turnberry's 17th hole. Seve Ballesteros suffered a crushing defeat at Turnberry in 1979 when Sandy Lyle birdied 6 of the first 7 holes on the way to a last round of 65 in the European Open. That catapulted Lyle to number one in the Order of Merit – a position Ballesteros had held from 1976-78.*

FAR RIGHT: *The phenomenal Seve Ballesteros splashes the ball out of this greenside bunker toward the hole.*

Yet even if Nicklaus has a high regard for Norman it would appear more likely that Ballesteros, with two Open Championship wins and two US Masters successes, is the man who was responsible for driving the biggest wedge between Nicklaus and Watson. The Spaniard sharpened his claws against the Golden Bear by pushing Nicklaus into joint second place at Royal Lytham and St Annes in 1979 and it was Watson who had to accept that position at St Andrews in 1984.

Ballesteros ushered in a new era. The young golfer from the north coast of Spain soon showed that he was the most exciting prospect since Arnold Palmer. As a 19-year-old he captured the imagination of the world with his brave bid to win the Open Championship at Royal Birkdale. After three rounds he took the lead, and in spite of eventually finishing

joint runner-up with Nicklaus behind Miller, he was here to stay. Later that year Ballesteros linked with his compatriot, Manuel Pinero, to win the World Cup for Spain – pushing the American combination of Jerry Pate who had won the US Open that summer at the Atlanta Athletic Club in Georgia, and Dave Stockton, the reigning US PGA champion, into second place at Mission Hills, California.

So two unknown Spaniards had hammered out an early warning to American golf. There was a revolutionary move in Europe with players on the continent emerging to challenge for the big prizes on offer in golf. That Ballesteros and Pinero should win the World Cup was quite remarkable. For instance Pinero, born in Badajoz near the Portuguese border, was a product of the caddie schools. His father was a pig farmer but when times became hard the family

ABOVE: *Seve Ballesteros, putter and ball in hand, in thought about the situation confronting him.*

RIGHT: *Jose-Maria Canizares of Spain in action during the Ryder Cup at Walton Heath, Surrey in 1981. He lost his singles match to Hale Irwin as the United States beat Europe 18½-9½.*

moved to Madrid, and so Pinero found his way to the Club de Campo course where he could earn a few pesetas to supplement the family income.

In Spain the game of golf was known only to the aristocracy who played at sophisticated clubs, and to the children of impoverished families who turned up to caddie. The origins of the game in Spain can be traced to British architects but the sport was virtually a private, exclusive pastime. The taxi-driver and the shop worker, the hotelier and the motor mechanic, knew nothing of the sport. For them the major pastimes were football and bullfighting.

The likes of Pinero, however, profited by working at golf clubs. On occasions they were allowed to borrow clubs from the members and so hone their own games. Even so it required enormous strength of character to survive. Yet there was an instinctive quality about the golf of some of these continental players. Ballesteros personifies this best although he had the advantage of coming from a golfing background. His uncle Ramon had proved himself to be a golfer of high regard by winning six Opens around the world. If you thumb your way back through the record books then you will see that in 1965 Ramon Sota succeeded in finishing sixth in the US Masters behind Jack Nicklaus!

Ballesteros had more than just background going for him. He had inherited an athletic ability from his father who, apart from being a fine long distance runner, rowed on several occasions in the Pedrena boat that won national championships in annual matches around Santander Bay. More importantly the Ballesteros home – a nineteenth century farmhouse – overlooked the Real Club de Golf de Pedrena, and his brothers, Baldomero, Manuel and Vicente, were all golfers. Even so it was far from easy for Ballesteros to develop his game.

For instance Seve hit his first shots at the age of seven with a club fashioned from a rusting three-iron head hand-fitted into a stick acting as a shaft. His ammunition? Stones that he collected from the nearby beach. Golf balls were too expensive for one so young. Ballesteros, like so many Spaniards who were to make a living from golf, initially caddied to earn his keep. Then at the age of ten he played in his first event. It was held over nine holes and Ballesteros carded a 51. Two years later he had become the caddie champion at Pedrena with the impressive score of 79. In 1973 he was once again the caddie champion although on this occasion he managed a score of 65. There was to be no stopping him and in January 1974 at the age of 16 years and eight months he became the youngest accredited professional in the history of Spanish golf.

What Ballesteros did was to assume the role of challenger to American golfers on their own soil. He was soon winning abroad and in 1977 he claimed both the Japanese Open and the Dunlop Phoenix, also staged in Japan. Ballesteros was hailed as a king in Japan where the interest in golf had been fueled by Japan's World Cup victory in 1957, whereas the success of Ballesteros and Pinero did not have an immediate impact on the game in Spain. There the likes of Ballesteros would have to resort to gimmicky productions such as hitting balls over the stands at the

RIGHT: *Seve Ballesteros with the Open Championship trophy which he won in 1979 and again in 1984.*

FAR RIGHT: *Seve Ballesteros sinks the putt on the 18th green which secured for him the Open title at St Andrews in 1984.*

BELOW: *Manuel Ballesteros, brother of Seve, jumps in the air as his ball rolls toward the hole at the third during the Martini Tournament at Wentworth, Surrey, in 1980.*

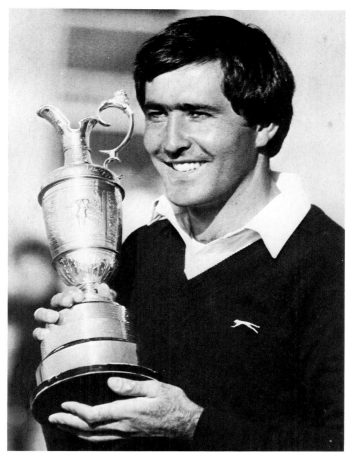

Bernabeu Stadium, the home of the Real Madrid Football Club, so as to spread the word to the populace. The public were admitted free of charge to their specially organized golf clinics.

In Japan the sport flourished even if many of those attracted to the game would never hit a golf ball on a course. Quite simply many of the millions of golf enthusiasts would be confined to the driving ranges because they could not afford the huge entry fees – up to $1.75 million at Koganei, Tokyo – for any of the 400 clubs.

Ballesteros, of course, enjoyed his victories in Japan. Even so he scored a far more significant success across the Pacific Ocean when, to acclimatize himself for the US Masters, he accepted an invitation to compete in the Great Greensboro Open in North Carolina. There was something Nicklaus-like in the manner in which Ballesteros, who survived the halfway cut by only one shot, came from ten strokes behind with rounds of 69 and 66 to win by one from Jack Renner and Fuzzy Zoeller. The impact that Ballesteros made in the United States cannot be overexaggerated. The following week at Augusta he was partnered on the last day with Gary Player who put together the 64 that would win him the Championship. Then next, at the Tournament of Champions, Ballesteros sped into the halfway lead only to falter with a closing 79 which enabled Player to come through and snatch victory once again.

RIGHT: *The incomparable Seve Ballesteros putting with his usual grace and flair.*

ABOVE: *Seve Ballesteros looks happy, but not so Tom Watson (right) as the 1983 US Masters unfolds, with the Spaniard on the way to victory.*

LEFT: *Fuzzy Zoeller, one of the most colorful characters in the game, has suffered for many years with a back condition that has restricted his winning chances.*

FAR LEFT: *Seve Ballesteros makes a club selection following consultation with his brother Vicente, caddying for him at the Westchester Classic in Rye, New York State.*

RIGHT: *Ben Crenshaw, who finally broke his major championship hoodoo by winning the US Masters in 1984.*

FAR RIGHT: *Ben Crenshaw playing in the 1979 Open Championship at Royal Lytham. He has said it will break his heart if he fails to win this championship before the end of his career.*

Player went on to win the Houston Open to complete a rare hat-trick. That streak, however, would be the start of the decline of Player's phenomenal career and it was Ballesteros who took up the baton. In 1980 he became only the second overseas golfer – following in Player's footsteps – to win the US Masters, and he did so with the greatest of ease. He was four ahead at the halfway stage, seven in front after 54 holes, and no fewer than 16 under par with a ten-shot lead midway through the final round. Eventually he won by only four shots – Gibby Gilbert and Australia's Jack Newton shared second spot – but it was still a masterful performance. He had become at the age of 23 the youngest champion in the history of the Masters. What is more he won the title again in 1983 when he accelerated away from Ben Crenshaw and Tom Kite in the final round to win by four shots.

What Ballesteros did with his smash-and-grab raids in the United States so the Australian Greg Norman matched with his more orthodox approach. Norman elected to play full time on the US circuit although it has to be emphasized that he married an American and that he found it easier to settle and live in Florida. The hardest aspect of a professional golfer's life is travel, and Ballesteros prefers to spend much of his time playing in his native Europe. Norman played on the European circuit for several seasons, heading the Order of Merit in 1982, before he decided it was time to move on to the greener pastures of the US Tour.

RIGHT: *Texan Tom Kite has earned the reputation of being the finest golfer in the modern-day game who has not won a major championship.*

Bernhard Langer of West Germany is another who has accepted the American way of life. He too married an American and he has stuck to the rules as far as the ownership of a US PGA Tour player's card is concerned. Langer, however, would like to see

LEFT: *Greg Norman, arms aloft, had every reason to celebrate in 1986. He won no fewer than ten tournaments that year, including the British Open Championship.*

these rules relaxed to encourage greater flexibility in the individual schedules of players worldwide. In winning the US Masters in 1985 he has proved himself a golfer of world class in the United States. There he has become only the third foreign player to wear the green jacket.

Langer's progress illustrates how public attitudes toward golf have changed in recent years. He recalls

that little more than 15 years ago – 1972 to be precise – he announced to his friends that he wanted to become a professional golfer. 'They thought I was mad and they had every right too,' said Langer. 'Even then I hardly knew of the existence of people like Jack Nicklaus and Arnold Palmer!'

That is hardly surprising. Bernhard, the son of a bricklayer, was born in the hamlet of Anheusen which

ABOVE: *Ben Crenshaw coaxes home another putt on his way to the US Masters title at Augusta in 1984.*

RIGHT: *Tom Kite illustrated his consistency as a golfer, when, in 1981, he won the Inverrary Classic, finished runner-up in three other events, third three times, fourth once and in the top six on no fewer than 14 occasions.*

FAR RIGHT: *Greg Norman celebrates with his caddy following his victory in the Open Championship at Turnberry in 1986.*

ABOVE: *Trouble for Greg Norman during the US Open at Shinnecock Hills in 1986 where he led after three rounds, then tumbled out of the reckoning.*

LEFT: *Bernhard Langer of West Germany receives congratulations from Ben Crenshaw and the green jacket following his US Masters triumph at Augusta in 1985.*

RIGHT: *Bernhard Langer hoods his hands over his eyes to cut out the glare of the sun and obtain a better idea of the putt he faces.*

FAR RIGHT: *A good example of the cross-handed method preferred by Bernhard Langer, who earlier in his career suffered a savage attack of the 'yips.' Here he sinks another putt on the slick Augusta greens on the way to becoming the first West German and only the third overseas player to win the US Masters.*

BELOW: *Bernhard Langer, whose love affair with the game of golf began at the age of nine when he became a caddy at the local Augsburg course, finds himself in deep trouble at a bush. His loyal caddy, Peter Coleman, looks on.*

at the time had a population of 1200. His father Erwin, one of the millions of refugees from Sudetenland in Czechoslovakia, was caught by Russians and put on a train which, presumably, was heading for Siberia. 'He jumped the train,' explained Bernhard. 'They shot at him, but they missed, and he walked all the way to Germany.' Bernhard, the youngest of three children, became a caddie at the age of nine at the Augsburg course in the village of Burgwalden. Langer possessed, however, that indefinable quality called ambition. To improve his own game he made sure that he caddied for the club champion. Then he moved on to be the assistant professional at Munich before joining the European Tour.

What threatened to end Langer's career before it had started was an attack of the putting yips. Call it the twitch, if you like, but this dreaded affliction which usually occurs in later life is the 'disease' that all golfers fear. That Langer has exorcized the demon from his game is in itself a minor miracle. There might be occasions when it returns to haunt him, but at Augusta where the greens are recognized to be the fastest in the world, he proved he could cope by winning the US Masters.

Nicklaus, at the age of 46, was to relieve Langer of the title in 1986, then two months later Raymond Floyd, at 43, became the oldest winner of the US Open. In a curious way these events highlighted the situation in which golf now found itself. Greg Norman and Bob Tway, a 27-year-old from Oklahoma City, were to score their first major championship successes in the Open Championship and the US PGA Championship respectively. Even so it seemed that the time when a single player could dominate the game of golf had now passed.

ABOVE: *Oklahoma City's Bob Tway enjoyed a memorable second season on the US Tour when he achieved four wins, including the US PGA Championship, and finished second in the Order of Merit, behind Greg Norman.*

LEFT: *At 6 feet 4 inches Bob Tway is one of the tallest professional golfers in the world. Because of his height and build he patterned his swing on that of Tom Weiskopf.*

FAR LEFT: *This putt missed, but most dropped for Raymond Floyd, when, at the age of 43, and with a dazzling last round of 66, he became at Shinnecock Hills in June 1986 the oldest US Open champion in history.*

ABOVE: *A magic moment for Chirstina Loran Floyd as she holds the US Open trophy won by her father Raymond (left) at Shinnecock Hills in June 1986. Raymond's wife, Maria, looks on.*

LEFT: *The time when individual golfers dominated appeared to be coming toward an end when the US PGA Championship was passed on from one player to another in the 1980s. Bob Tway, winner in 1986, is seen doing his level best to imitate a football player.*

FAR LEFT: *A panoramic shot of Shinnecock Hills, scene of the US Open in 1986.*

RIGHT: *Newcomers won the first three of the four majors in 1987, but Larry Nelson changed that trend with his success in the US PGA Championship at the PGA National Champion's Course, Palm Beach Gardens, Florida, where he beat Lanny Wadkins in a play-off.*

FAR RIGHT: *Andy North holds a unique record, because after winning the US Open in 1978 he did not win another championship until the US Open in 1985.*

BELOW: *Larry Nelson won the US PGA Championship for the first time in his career in 1981 and regained it six years later in 1987.*

Except for the two victories of Ballesteros the US Masters had spent most of its time in the 1980s in different hands. From 1980 to 1986 the US Open winners were Jack Nicklaus, David Graham, Tom Watson, Larry Nelson, Fuzzy Zoeller, Andy North and Ray Floyd. During that time the US PGA Championship was handed on by Nicklaus to Nelson to Floyd to Hal Sutton to Trevino to Green and then to Tway. True, Tom Watson did win the Open Championship in 1980, 1982 and 1983. Even so, Bill Rogers (1981), Ballesteros (1984), Sandy Lyle (1985) and Norman were the other winners.

The curtain had descended on a dominant force. Further evidence of that came in 1987, the 'Year of the Newcomers,' with Larry Mize (US Masters), Scott Simpson (US Open) and Nick Faldo (Open Championship) all winning majors for the first time, until Larry Nelson interrupted the sequence with his success in the US PGA Championship in the steamy heat of Florida. It is a fact that in 1969 all the major championships were won by first-time winners, with George Archer (US Masters), Orville Moody (US Open), Tony Jacklin (Open Championship) and Ray Floyd (US PGA Championship) scooping the honors that year. That, however, was one of those rare years when Nicklaus did not rule.

ABOVE: *Texan Bill Rogers clenches his fist and salutes supporters following his 1981 British Open triumph.*

ABOVE LEFT: *Hubert Green, who won the US Open in 1977 and the US PGA Championship in 1985, might have won the US Masters in 1978 had not this three-foot putt missed on the last green at Augusta.*

LEFT: *Hal Sutton, who won the US Amateur Championship in 1980, made a successful switch to the professional ranks by winning the US PGA Championship in 1983.*

FAR LEFT: *Orville Moody was the reigning US Open champion when he participated in the British Open at Royal Lytham and St Annes in 1969.*

ABOVE: *Jerry Pate, who won the US Open in 1976, plunged into the lake following his 1982 win in the Tournament Players Championship at the Tournament Players Club at Sawgrass in Florida.*

RIGHT: *Larry Mize plays from a bunker at the 18th hole during the 1987 US Masters which he won following a play-off.*

FAR RIGHT: *A jump of joy from Larry Mize. He is celebrating a 60-yard pitch shot that disappeared into the hole for a birdie at the second extra hole in the 1987 US Masters play-off. Mize beat both Seve Ballesteros and Greg Norman.*

ABOVE: *Nick Faldo, who won the British Open in 1987, later led England to victory, in the Dunhill Cup at St Andrews.*

LEFT: *Nick Faldo settles down for a photo session with his wife Gill and their daughter Natalie following his Open Championship triumph at Muirfield in 1987. With his win Faldo became the second British winner of the Championship in three years, following Sandy Lyle's success in 1983.*

RIGHT: *Nick Faldo, who won the Sea Pines Heritage Classic on the US Tour in 1984, studies a putt on the way to his British Open victory at Muirfield in 1987.*

FAR RIGHT: *Californian Scott Simpson was pressed all the way by Tom Watson but he courageously held on to win the US Open in 1987 at the Olympic Club, San Francisco.*

BELOW LEFT: *Teacher David Leadbetter (left), seen here with Mark Lye, also taught Nick Faldo. After winning the 1987 British Open at Muirfield, Faldo praised Leadbetter for his fine tuition.*

BELOW RIGHT *Lanny Wadkins' club flies into the air. He can hardly believe his misfortune, but 1987 was not to be his year again as he was beaten in a play-off for the US PGA Championship by Larry Nelson.*

Even so the newcomers of 1987 certainly showed their spirit by nailing their opponents with strokes of sheer brilliance even if they enjoyed a touch of luck. Gary Player, however, insisted that the harder you work, the luckier you get.

At Augusta it was the hometown boy Mize who produced the most theatrical finish, with a dance of delight, as he holed out with a one-million-to-one shot at the second extra hole. That torpedoed Greg Norman after Seve Ballesteros had sunk himself by taking three putts at the first extra hole of their play-off. Next it was Simpson's turn to sabotage a super-star as he parried Tom Watson's brave charge in the US Open at the Olympic Club, San Francisco. It might have been Watson again in the Open Championship at Muirfield, but Faldo, with 18 successive pars in the final round, provided Britain with much to celebrate following Lyle's success in that champion-ship two years earlier.

Quite rightly Nelson now insists that he deserves more recognition, especially after his play-off success over Lanny Wadkins in the US PGA Championship when he gained his third major championship. That's two more than Norman who reputedly earns in the

region of $20 million each year, and only one less than Ballesteros who cannot be too far behind his Australian rival in the earning stakes.

Ballesteros and Norman, however, possess the charisma as well as the class. Walter Hagen had it and so did Henry Cotton. And as superstars, it is inevit-able that they should benefit more than others. The big money has attracted a new style of player to the game. In Europe the tour remained for a long time a social event. When you finished a round you retired to the bar. The game bred characters but it didn't breed world-class winners.

With the increase in prize money in Europe – up from £1.3 million in 1980 to £10 million in 1988 – came a new player. Nick Faldo became only the third British player to win on the US Tour – following in the footsteps of Tony Jacklin and Peter Oosterhuis (Canadian Open) – when he took the Sea Pines Heri-tage Classic in 1984. Then it was Sandy Lyle's turn at the Greater Greensboro Open in 1986 and then again at the Tournament Players Championship in 1987. Ken Brown followed that with his win in the South-ern Open in 1987.

The pendulum had swung again.

ABOVE: *Ken Brown has played the US Tour on a full-time basis since 1984, and his dedication and devotion finally reaped a rich reward when in 1987 he won the Southern Open at Green Island Country Club, Columbus, Georgia. In 1986 Brown had made only a handful of visits to his native British circuit, and here he is pictured playing in the European Open at Sunningdale when he lost in a play-off to Greg Norman.*

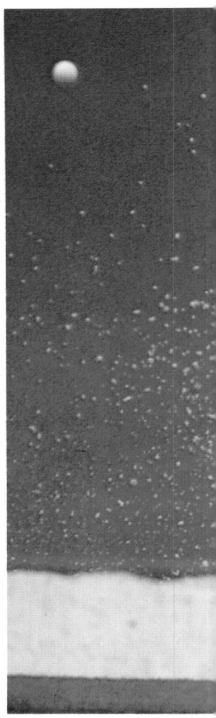

LEFT: *For Sandy Lyle this was truly a moment to treasure: he kisses the British Open trophy following his win at Royal St George's in 1985 when he became the first British winner since Tony Jacklin in 1969.*

FAR LEFT: *A happy Ken Brown displays the trophies that he won at the Four Stars Tournament on the PGA European Tour at Moor Park, England in 1985.*

ABOVE LEFT: *Scott Simpson holds the US Open trophy following his win in 1987, while his wife Cheryl grasps the 18th hole flag at San Francisco's Olympic Club.*

ABOVE: *Sandy Lyle is reckoned to have the game to win the US Masters at Augusta. He has certainly proved his winning capabilities on American soil with successes in the Greater Greensboro Open in 1986 and the Tournament Players Championship in 1987.*

LEFT: *Sandy Lyle celebrates following his win in the British Open at Royal St George's, England in 1985. Michael Bonallack, Secretary of the Royal and Ancient, holds the silver claret jug.*

Stars of Tomorrow

LEFT: *Severiano Ballesteros (left) of Spain won the US Masters in 1980 and 1983. On this occasion in 1985, however, he had to settle for a share of second place as West Germany's Bernhard Langer, whom Seve is congratulating here on the last green at Augusta, triumphed. Ballesteros and Langer detonated a new golfing explosion, this time on the continent of Europe, where a plethora of new stars emerged.*

RIGHT: *The Ryder Cup trophy, which was held by the United States from 1957 until 1985, when Europe won at The Belfry, England.*

The finest barometer for measuring the immediate future of the game must be the Ryder Cup. Since the early days, the Ryder Cup has been dominated by the United States. The contest was inaugurated in 1927, following two unofficial matches, and the United States and Great Britain gained two wins apiece in the first four encounters of this biennial affair. Subsequently the United States became the dominant force in the game. There was little for Great Britain to cheer about as the British team waited from 1933 to 1957 for another win. That year Dai Rees led them to victory at Lindrick.

Thereafter the United States resumed command. America continued to win with consummate ease, except for a tie at Royal Birkdale in 1969, and it was feared in some quarters that the contest would become extinct unless it was revitalized. It was Jack Nicklaus who approached Lord Derby, the President of the British PGA, with the suggestion that the inclusion of players from the continent of Europe might foster a new beginning for the match. Nicklaus did not want the Ryder Cup to die and he was concerned that it might. Consequently the British PGA convened a special committee meeting at which it was decided to vary the Deed of Trust, with the result that Nicklaus's suggestion was sanctioned.

Initially it did not appear to make a scrap of difference. Severiano Ballesteros and Antonio Garrido, both of Spain, were included in the European team in 1979 but they lost heavily by 17-11 at the Greenbrier in West Virginia. There was to be an even more humiliating reversal for the Europeans two years later when on home territory at Walton Heath in Surrey they went down 18½-9½. Europe, however, excluded Seve Ballesteros because at the time he was locked in a bitter wrangle with the PGA over appearance money. The United States sent over twelve outstanding players to participate in the contest.

ABOVE: *Samuel Ryder, a St Albans seed merchant and donor of the Ryder Cup, photographed in May 1927 when the first of the biennial matches between Great Britain and the United States was staged.*

RIGHT: *Samuel Ryder (left) presents the Ryder Cup to George Duncan, Great Britain's captain, after the United States had lost 7-5 at Moortown, Leeds in 1929.*

ABOVE: *Another intriguing Ryder Cup encounter reaches its conclusion and this time both captains – America's Sam Snead (left) and Britain's Eric Brown – have something to smile about as the 1969 encounter at Royal Birkdale finishes in a 16-16 draw.*

ABOVE LEFT: *A busy day for the signwriter in June 1933 as he keeps everybody at the Southport and Ainsdale Club in Lancashire aware of the positions in the Ryder Cup match.*

LEFT: *Dai Rees certainly played a captain's role at Lindrick, Sheffield, in 1957 when he gained two points out of two as Britain beat the United States 7½-4½.*

The team consisted of Jack Nicklaus, Tom Watson, Lee Trevino, Ray Floyd, Johnny Miller, Tom Kite, Ben Crenshaw, Hale Irwin, Jerry Pate, Bill Rogers, Bruce Leitzke and Larry Nelson. The European team, with Ballesteros absent and Jacklin also excluded for the first time since 1967, did not have the winner of a major championship in their squad. It was like taking lambs to the slaughter.

Yet there was a growing sense of achievement in Europe. Ballesteros, in spite of his confrontations with officialdom, had matured into the finest player in the world. He did not, of course, possess the record of Nicklaus but he could, on the day, take on any player with the belief that he was the favorite to win. By dint of his record in the United States and around the world, he set an example for his European colleagues. Thus with Ballesteros's encouragement and the inspiration of Jacklin, now the captain, Europe came within a whisker of winning the 1983 contest at the PGA National Golf Club at Palm Beach Gardens, Florida. There, with Nicklaus in charge, the United States squeezed home by 14½-13½.

There was cause to celebrate as far as Europe was concerned, because this result unquestionably raised the possibility of victory being attained at The Belfry, Sutton Coldfield, in 1985. By now Ballesteros was the winner of four major championships, and during 1985 Bernhard Langer had won the US Masters while Sandy Lyle had become the first British player since Jacklin in 1969 to win the Open Championship. With Jacklin once more at the helm there was such confidence in the European camp that the American team, led on this occasion by Lee Trevino, suffered a shattering blow to their pride when they were beaten 16½-11½. There were now four Spaniards in the team – Ballesteros, Jose-Maria Canizares, Pinero and Jose Rivero – and little Pinero exemplified the determination among the Europeans by leading off in the singles to beat Lanny Wadkins.

Many observers of this exciting game were in agreement at the time that the match swung on a putt of little more than 15 inches that Craig Stadler had missed on the last green in the fourballs on the second morning. That cost the Americans the lead which they would never regain. In retrospect Stadler's alarming miss might be regarded as the moment when the pendulum swung. Most certainly it lit the blue touch paper on another explosive boom, with the PGA European Tour growing in strength as an increasing number of sponsors, especially on the continent, stampeded their way onto the scene.

With the onrush of money – the Tour's overall purse multiplied nearly tenfold between 1980 and 1988 – came a new breed of player. Suddenly the practice grounds of Europe were frequented like those in the United States. More golfers from other countries, especially Australia, joined the circuit, and this helped to heighten competition. Countries on the European continent too were producing more golfers. For instance in Sweden there had begun one of the most disciplined training programs in the history of sport. Jan Blomquist had been charged with raising the standing of golf to such a degree that Sweden could be as proud of their golfers as they were of their tennis players such as Bjorn Borg.

LEFT: *Jose-Maria Canizares was one of four Spanish players in the European team that won the Ryder Cup at The Belfry, England, in 1985.*

BELOW LEFT: *Craig Stadler, the burly American, could not believe his misfortune when he missed a 15-inch putt on the last green in the fourballs on the second morning. It was a miss that shook the confidence of the American team and galvanized the Europeans toward a historic triumph.*

FAR LEFT ABOVE: *Bernhard Langer of West Germany celebrates as a vital putt drops during the 1985 Ryder Cup at The Belfry, England, which Europe won by 16½ points to 11½ against the United States.*

FAR LEFT BELOW: *Europe's triumphant Ryder Cup team in 1985 was (left to right): Back row: Sam Torrance, Severiano Ballesteros, Ken Brown, Nick Faldo, Sandy Lyle, Howard Clark, Jose-Maria Canizares, Manuel Pinero. Front row: Paul Way, Ian Woosnam, Tony Jacklin (captain), Bernhard Langer, Jose Rivero.*

RIGHT: *Mats Lanner, one of Sweden's emerging players, captured the Epson Grand Prix at the St Pierre Country Club, Chepstow, Wales in May 1987, and in the process landed a £50,000 prize.*

FAR RIGHT: *Ove Sellberg became the first Swedish player to win on the PGA European Tour by taking the Epson Grand Prix title in 1986.*

FAR RIGHT BELOW: *Anders Forsbrand finished eighth in the PGA European Order of Merit in 1986 and he confirmed his talent by winning the European Masters in 1987.*

In 1980 Blomquist took a team of Swedes to the Eisenhower Trophy, the world amateur team championship, and they were palpably outclassed. The United States won, with Sweden trailing home eighth, more than 40 strokes behind. Blomquist stuck to his guns and he implemented a training program that included a strict diet, no alcohol, weight-training and psychological talks. In 1982 Sweden finished second to the United States in the Eisenhower Trophy and Ove Sellberg, a member of that team, became in 1986 the first Swedish player to win on the PGA European Tour. He won the Epson Grand Prix, a match-play event, at the St Pierre Country Club, Chepstow, and twelve months later his successor was his compatriot Mats Lanner.

Jacklin had predicted following the Ryder Cup match at The Belfry in 1985 that the next European team would contain a Swedish player. However, although Anders Forsbrand, another Swedish player, won the European Masters at Crans-sur-Sierre, Switzerland, he was too late to earn a place in the 1987 team.

In 1987 the European team produced the most telling result in the history of the competition. A team of four Scotsmen, three Spaniards, two Englishmen, one Irishman, one Welshman and one West German linked together to win on American soil for the first

PREVIOUS PAGES: *The Belfry, home of the British PGA, was the scene of Europe's Ryder Cup win over the United States in 1985. There the Brabazon course, set in parkland, has developed into one of England's premiere inland courses.*

ABOVE: *Bernhard Langer keeps Europe on a roll in the Ryder Cup at the Belfry in 1985 by holing out from a bunker.*

time. The score of 15-13 is a minor consideration. For Tony Jacklin and Jack Nicklaus, the respective European and American captains, it was a watershed in the game.

Jacklin and Nicklaus voiced their agreement following the end of the match that Europe's success could change the face of world golf. Nicklaus had announced prior to the match that he felt that his team as a whole had greater strength and that the European team was still very much the underdog. He clearly considered the American team to have a supreme advantage with the match being contested on the course that he had built at Muirfield Village. Once the match was over he acknowledged that the time had come for the United States to eliminate archaic rules that not only restrict the number of international players allowed to compete on their circuit but also reduce the competitive nature of American players.

Nicklaus has campaigned longer than one can remember for less stringent rules. He is unhappy that a player of the caliber of Severiano Ballesteros must meet certain conditions in order to select where and when he wishes to compete on the US Tour. By not accepting full membership – a condition of which is that a player competes in a minimum of 15 US events – the Spaniard has been restricted to five appearances plus the major championships.

ABOVE: *Europe's 1987 winning Ryder Cup team celebrates, following their victory over the American team at Muirfield Village, Columbus, Ohio. Standing left to right are Seve Ballesteros, Gordon Brand Junior, Sandy Lyle, Tony Jacklin, Nick Faldo, Sam Torrance, Eamonn Darcy. Front row, left to right: Jose Rivero, Jose-Maria Olazabal, Ken Brown, Ian Woosnam, Bernhard Langer, Howard Clark.*

RIGHT: *Celebration time following Europe's victory over the United States in the 1987 Ryder Cup, with (left to right) Sam Torrance, Nick Faldo and Ian Woosnam joining in the festivities.*

PREVIOUS PAGES: *The opening ceremony of the 1987 Ryder Cup match between the United States and Europe, where the Ohio State Band enlivened proceedings on the course Jack Nicklaus built at Muirfield Village.*

Nicklaus's point of view, however, has been swamped by that of the majority of American professionals. They have virtually condemned Nicklaus for trying to change a system that works and provides them with a good living. Nicklaus, however, is looking toward the future. 'Look, it's simple: without the stars you don't have a tour. All sports need their heroes, their superstars, and we need them in golf in the United States as much as they are needed in Europe.'

In essence Nicklaus would like to see the leading players on all the tours – Australia, Europe, Japan and the United States – encouraged to compete wherever and whenever they wish with the proviso that they satisfy the requirements of their own tour. 'I think we should allow competition to thrive internationally rather than stifle it,' he added.

It will require some radical motivators alongside Nicklaus to alter the current policies of the US Tour. Yet they need only look across the Atlantic to see how the European scene has benefited from opening the doors to international golfers. For instance American golfers, who have been encouraged historically to compete, have been enticed by lucrative arrangements, commonly known in the trade as appearance money. The presence of a Ben Crenshaw at an Italian Open or a Johnny Miller at a Scandinavian Open has assisted the growth in the sport in those countries.

In future years American golfers may regard playing in more overseas tournaments as beneficial to their game. There is a growing belief that the United States colleges, the traditional grooming grounds of the American golfers, may be playing their part in producing golfing automata. What is more the US Tour has leaned heavily toward 'stadium' courses, which are first class for spectators, but possibly rather too similar to be able offer the golfer any real opportunity of widening his repertoire of shots.

LEFT: *A happy Tony Jacklin with the Ryder Cup receives congratulations from Lord Derby, President of the British PGA, following Europe's success in 1987. J R Carpenter, President of the US PGA, is on the right.*

BELOW LEFT: *Ken Schofield, who in his role as Secretary of the PGA European Tour, took prize money for the 1988 season to a record £10,000,000.*

BELOW: *Texan Ben Crenshaw made several visits to Europe in the 1970s at a time when many Amerian golfers, enticed by appearance money, helped to assist the golf boom in Britain on the continent of Europe.*

RIGHT: *Curtis Strange, top of the US PGA Tour Order of Merit in 1985, led the money list again in 1987 with a record $925,941.*

FAR RIGHT: *Most golfing observers considered Ian Woosnam to be the player of the year in 1987 when he won eight tournaments. His wins included the Suntory World Match-Play Championship, of which he was the first British winner.*

BELOW: *Ian Woosnam escapes from a bunker during the final of the Suntory World Match-Play Championship at Wentworth in 1987 in which he beat Sandy Lyle. Woosnam, who at 5 feet 4½ inches is one of the shortest players in the world, also led the European Order of Merit with record winnings of £253,717.*

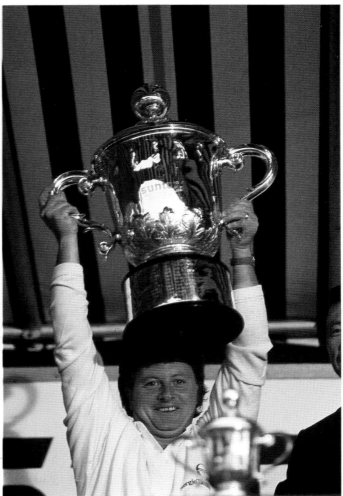

The growth of the game in Europe has led to the schedule taking in a greater variety of courses so that golfers such as Ballesteros and Langer, Faldo and Lyle, have learned to improvise whereas Curtis Strange and Payne Stewart, Ben Crenshaw and Lanny Wadkins, are compelled to play target golf.

The American team recovered from its setback in the Ryder Cup to win the Kirin Cup in Japan. Even so there were other notable results in 1987 which suggested that the United States can no longer claim world supremacy. The World Match-Play Championship, now sponsored by Suntory, is an annual affair staged at Wentworth each autumn that brings together the cream of world golf. Palmer and Player dominated the championship for five years following its inception in 1964, and in recent times Ballesteros and Norman have reigned supreme.

Ian Woosnam broke their monopoly when in the final in 1987 he overcame Sandy Lyle to become the first British winner of the Championship. Woosnam was also the number one player on the European Order of Merit, with winnings of £253,717, while Curtis Strange led in the US with $925,941.

If it seems short-sighted to continually compare Europe with the United States then that is not to say that Japanese golfers, for instance, are not prospering. The game of golf has become a national pastime around the globe and its popularity will continue to grow. The tours in Australia and New Zealand and South Africa might not have such lucrative foundations as those in Europe, Japan and the United States but they still encourage participation in the sport by providing a shop window for their own golfers.

The Sony World Rankings, which are sanctioned by the Royal and Ancient Golf Club of St Andrews, are now accepted in most quarters as a commonsense guide to the individual strengths of golfers. So while Greg Norman, Severiano Ballesteros and Bernhard Langer remain in the leading three places so American golfers continue to have strength as a whole. On 1 January 1985, before their two Ryder Cup defeats, the United States had 56 players in the top 100. By 1 November 1987 that number had risen to 60. Even so there has been a change in the leading 25, with the American contingent falling from 17 to 13. Europe's entry has remained unchanged at five with Japan's increased from two to three, Australia's from one to two and South Africa's from none to two.

The South African connection is interesting. Mark McNulty, following three unsatisfactory seasons on the US Tour, elected to return to compete in Europe in 1985. At that time he was ranked 185th in the world. By the end of the 1987 season – he finished second to Woosnam in the official money list – McNulty had risen to seventh place. In the meantime David Frost, a South African compatriot of McNulty, had climbed to 11th place in the US Tour money list in 1987. He won $518,072 compared with McNulty's haul of £189,303. Yet McNulty is recognized as a 'winner' – he has scored no fewer than 14 successes in two years – whereas Frost is still seeking that first elusive win on the US Tour. In other words, as Nicklaus pointed out, it is possible to become rich very quickly on the dollar-laden fairways of the American circuit without actually becoming a winner.

ABOVE: *Tommy Nakajima of Japan splashes out of a bunker.*

LEFT: *Tommy Nakajima decides a flat cap is the order of the day for the 1986 Dunhill Cup which was played at St Andrews in Scotland.*

RIGHT: *Calvin Peete in action for the United States against Europe in the 1983 Ryder Cup match at the PGA National Golf Club, Palm Beach Gardens, Florida, in October 1983.*

BELOW: *Calvin Peete, who until the age of 23 had no intention of 'chasing a little ball around under a hot sun,' lines up a putt and thinks about the $2 million he has earned in prize winnings alone since turning professional in 1976.*

What is certain is that the state of the game has rarely been healthier. Even the US PGA Seniors Tour has prospered in a manner few could have predicted. Al Geiberger, a Californian famous for shooting a record 59 in the Memphis Classic on the 7249-yard Colonial Country Club course in 1977, reached the magical age of 50 during the 1987 season. In six weeks he earned an astonishing $197,671 and there was more to come. That tour has benefited because of the presence of such colorful personalities as Arnold Palmer, Bill Casper, Doug Sanders and Chi Chi Rodriguez, with others including Bruce Crampton, Gary Player and Peter Thomson.

It is the regular tour that requires an injection of life. Jack Nicklaus cannot go on forever although Tom Watson, who achieved his first win for three years, and his largest ever pay check of $360,000 when he won the Nabisco Championship of Golf at Oak Hills Country Club, San Antonio, Texas, on 1 November 1987, might be back. There would be much to look forward to if a revitalized Watson went head-to-head with the likes of Ballesteros, Langer and Norman.

That apart, America must look for a new messiah on the fairways. Paul Azinger has made startling progress in the last two years, climbing in that time from outside the leading 200 to 12th place in the Sony Rankings, and he was a touch unfortunate not to win the Open Championship at Muirfield which Nick Faldo took. If Azinger can look upon that as a learning experience then, with the three successes that he scored on the US Tour in 1987, he could take himself to the forefront of the pack. Keith Clearwater is another with the potential to make his mark. With his win in the Centel Classic at the end of the 1987 season he took his winnings to $320,007, a figure that represents a record for a tour 'rookie' and which eclipsed the previous record of $260,536.

RIGHT: *Baldovino Dassu of Italy was one of the first players from the European continent to make his mark on the modern game. He set a record for Europe, with his low score of 60 for an 18-hole round in the Swiss Open at Crans-sur-Sierre in 1971.*

FAR RIGHT: *Al Geiberger took the US Seniors Tour by storm in 1987 after celebrating his fiftieth birthday. But he is still best remembered for the 59 he scored in the Memphis Classic on the Colonial Country Club course in 1977.*

BELOW: *Mark McNulty of South Africa, a prolific winner, was runner-up to Ian Woosnam in the 1987 European Order of Merit.*

LEFT: *Paul Azinger, playing here in the 1987 Masters, won three times on the US Tour and was named Player of the Year in 1987.*

BELOW LEFT: *Jumbo Ozaki is one of the leading players in Japan, where their golf boom has meant that the cost of club membership has risen out of all proportion compared with the rest of the world.*

FAR LEFT: *Gleneagles Golf Club has one of the most picturesque settings in the world and is now the home of the Bell's Scottish Open, which in 1987 was won by Ian Woosnam.*

LEFT: *Bernhard Langer's achievements have popularized the game in West Germany.*

BELOW: *Howard Clark scored a decisive win over Dan Pohl as Europe overcame the United States in the 1987 Ryder Cup Match.*

RIGHT: *Gordon Brand Junior, seen here recovering from the rough during the 1985 European Open, made his debut for Europe in the Ryder Cup in 1987.*

There are many American observers who regard Payne Stewart as the natural successor to the number one spot. The 'old guard' of Curtis Strange, Ben Crenshaw, Lanny Wadkins and Fuzzy Zoeller will continue to have their moments, as will the likes of Howard Clark and Sam Torrance in Europe. Nick Faldo and Sandy Lyle are well aware that they are being pressed by newcomers such as Gordon Brand Junior and Robert Lee. Greg Norman is head-and-shoulders above his Australian colleagues although Ian Baker-Finch has the potential to rival Rodger Davis for second spot, along with the improving Peter Senior. Tommy Nakajima is likely to remain Japan's number one as Isao Aoki gently drops away and Jumbo Ozaki makes the most significant progress.

However the flame lit by Severiano Ballesteros and Bernhard Langer continues to burn brightly, for it is on the continent of Europe that progress is likely to be made more quickly than anywhere else around the world. Jose-Maria Olazabal is the latest Spaniard to make his mark on the game – he formed an outstanding partnership with Ballesteros in the 1987 Ryder Cup – and Oliver Eckstein from West Germany looks capable of following in Bernhard Langer's footsteps. With the building of more courses the game will continue to increase in popularity. And significantly, Arnold Palmer, the man who galvanized the game, has said: 'The boom still really isn't on in Europe. It's only just about to happen.'

LEFT: *Tony Jacklin (left) and Seve Ballesteros salute the fans following Europe's first ever win in a Ryder Cup match on American soil in 1987. Jacklin was appointed to serve a fourth time as captain for the 1989 match at The Belfry, England.*

BELOW LEFT: *The sartorially elegant Payne Stewart, complete with plus-fours and matching cap and shoes, coaxes home a putt.*

BELOW RIGHT: *Sam Torrance was in the European Ryder Cup team again in 1987 following the 1985 match when he had the pleasure of sinking the putt on the last day of The Belfry – to assure Europe of their first win since 1957.*

OVERLEAF: *Spaniards Seve Ballesteros and Jose-Maria Olazabal celebrate as they win another vital point for Europe in the Ryder Cup match of 1987. For the first time in history the American team was beaten on home soil. It was a result which left Europe in ecstasy and America in agony. Both Tony Jacklin and Jack Nicklaus, the respective captains of the European and American teams, agreed that the result would have profound affect on world golf as it moved toward the twenty-first century.*

Index

Acknowledgements

The publisher would like to thank Adrian Hodgkins who designed this book; Melanie Earnshaw, the picture researcher; and Ron Watson, the indexer. We would also like to thank the following picture agencies and individuals for supplying illustrations (B = bottom, C = center, L = left, R = right, T = top):

All-Sport: pages 2-3, 16TL, 55CR, 75T, 78, 90L&BR, 91, 100T, 106-107, 111(below), 114L, 118, 119B, 123B, 137B, 139B, 146, 147, 150, 155B, 156B, 158, 162BR, 163T, 164TR&B, 166(all 3), 167T, 168, 172T, 173T, 174-175, 176(top 2), 177, 178-179, 181(both), 182(all 3), 183(both), 185TL&B, 186, 187(both), 188(below L), 188-189T, 189(below R), 190-191.
Associated Press: pages 38B, 50B, 64BR, 65T, 69T, 94T&BL, 100-101BC, 104R&B, 109B, 113(both), 116B, 117, 125L, 126B, 170B.
BBC Hulton Picture Library: pages 1, 8, 9, 12TR&B, 13, 16TR, 17B, 20B, 24, 27BL, 28, 28-29T, 29C&BL, 30TR&B, 31(both), 32BL, 33(both), 34(all 3), 38T, 44R, 45(both), 46, 47T, 49T&BL, 51T&CL, 52B, 57, 58R, 58-59T, 66B, 67BL, 69B, 70T, 73T, 76T, 79(both), 80(all 3), 81(both), 82 T&BC, 84T, 92-93B, 97BL, 121T, 125R, 145R, 148T.
The Bettmann Archive: pages 40, 41, 47B.
Peter Dazeley: pages 67TL&BR, 75B, 85BR, 87T&BR, 88T&L, 90TR, 92(both top), 93B, 95T, 97(top 2), 98, 101T, 103, 108B, 109T, 110, 111TR, 120, 121B, 124(both), 125T, 132(both), 133R, 134, 135B, 139T, 140, 141(main picture), 142, 144B, 145L, 149T&R, 151T&BL, 152(all 3), 153, 154BL, 157T, 160(both top), 161TL, 169, 184B, 185TR, 188TL.
Golf Illustrated: pages 26T, 27BR, 37B, 51R, 61T.
The Illustrated London News Picture Library: pages 32TR, 42BL.
The Keystone Collection: pages 4-5, 21B, 29BR, 36BR, 36-37T, 50T, 51B, 52T, 56, 58L, 59, 68B, 72, 73B, 74B, 76B, 77(all 3), 82BL, 83T, 84B, 85T&BL, 88BR, 94BR, 96, 100B, 101BR, 104L, 108L, 112B, 116(both top), 126T, 128, 129L, 148B, 149B, 161TR&BL, 170T, 171(all 3).
The Mansell Collection: page 32BR.
Brian Morgan, Golf Photography International: pages 30TL, 66T, 71, 74T, 87BL, 89(both), 95B, 99, 102(both), 105T, 114-115, 119(both top), 122(both top), 127, 130(below), 131, 137T, 141(inset), 143, 144T, 151BR, 154T&BR, 155T, 156(both top), 157(both below), 159(both), 160B, 161BR, 162TR&BL, 163B, 164AL&B, 165, 167B, 172B, 173B, 176B, 184T, 188BR, 189L.
The National Gallery, London: page 11.
National Railway Museum, York: page 6.
Peter Newark's Historical Pictures: page 14T.
William S Paton: pages 123T, 130T, 135, 136B.
S&G Press Agency: pages 39, 68TR, 105B, 111TL.
St. Andrews University Photographic Collection: pages 14B, 16B, 17T, 18(both), 19(both L), 20T&C, 22(both), 23, 25, 26B, 27T.
The Scotsman Publications: pages 55BL, 136T.
Scottish National Galleries: pages 10T, 12TL.
Scottish National Portrait Gallery: page 15.
UPI/Bettmann: pages 53B, 54, 55T, 63TL&B, 64L&TR, 65B, 86(both), 93T.
US Golf Association: pages 36L, 42(main picture), 43, 63TR, 68TL, 70B, 112(both top), 129R, 133L.
Weidenfeld Publishers: page 16B.
World Golf Hall of Fame: pages 44L, 49BR.